7 ESSENTIAL STRATEGIES OF AN EFFECTIVE GO-GETTER MOM

Habits of Highly Effective Entrepreneur Women

By

Tiffany Hudson

© **Copyright 2021 by Tiffany Hudson**

All rights reserved.

The content contained within this book may not be reproduced, duplicated or transmitted without direct written permission from the author or the publisher.

Under no circumstances will any blame or legal responsibility be held against the publisher, or author, for any damages, reparation, or monetary loss due to the information contained within this book, either directly or indirectly.

Legal Notice:

This book is copyright protected. It is only for personal use. You cannot amend, distribute, sell, use, quote or paraphrase any part, or the content within this book, without the consent of the author or publisher.

Disclaimer Notice:

Please note the information contained within this document is for educational and entertainment purposes only. All effort has been executed to present accurate, up to date, reliable, complete information. No warranties of any kind are declared or implied. Readers acknowledge that the author is not engaged in the rendering of legal, financial, medical or professional advice. The content within this book has been derived from various sources. Please consult a licensed professional before attempting any techniques outlined in this book.

By reading this document, the reader agrees that under no circumstances is the author responsible for any losses, direct or indirect, that are incurred as a result of the use of the information contained within this document, including, but not limited to, errors, omissions, or inaccuracies.

Table of Contents

Introduction 1
ChapteR 1: You Can Do It All—Know Your Limits 5
   How to Avoid Burnout 6
      Signs That You Have Burnout 7
      Tips That Help 10
      Accepting Help 12
Chapter 2: Finding Your Purpose 19
   Steps You Can Take 20
Chapter 3: Making It Happen 33
   Creating Your Action Plan 34
Chapter 4: Managing Your Goals 47
   Personal vs. Professional 48
      Personal Goals: What Are They? 48
      Professional Goals: What Are They? 51
   How to Focus On All Your Goals 54
Chapter 5: Define Your Own Meaning of "Great" 61
   Avoiding Bad Influences 61
   Achieving Greatness 68
Chapter 6: Boundaries: How to Set Them 75
   Household Boundaries 75
   Workplace Boundaries 80

Chapter 7: Clarifying Your Emotions 90
    Steps to Take 91
    The Key Points 98
    Why This Benefits You 100
Conclusion 105
References 107

INTRODUCTION

Being a mom is equivalent to being a superhero. You come to the rescue, always ready to tackle any challenges that you must face. Your children need you for guidance and nurturing. No matter what happens, the good and the bad, you are always there for them and there to listen. This nurturing aspect comes naturally to you, and you like to show it whenever you can. On the other side, you are a career-driven, powerful woman. Being given a list of tasks is like being told that you are about to run a race you know you can win. You excel at what you do, and you are great at staying motivated. Many women feel this way at some point, but more often than not, the question becomes how you will balance it all. Can you be a go-getter mom while also having a career path of your own to pursue?

The answer is yes: You can have both! This is not too good to be true because it requires plenty of hard work. You already know what this feels like—juggling multiple tasks at once. This book is here to guide you when you feel like giving up. When life gives you challenges, you will learn how to face them head-on. The techniques and methods you are about to learn will show you that you do not have to make a choice or an immediate sacrifice. You can be the nurturing and present mother that you have always been while growing a strong and steady career for yourself. This is what it means to be a go-getter, and you are going to succeed.

In society, women are expected to handle everything. When something goes wrong, it feels like it is up to us to make sure everything goes smoothly again. Even though you can do it all, this never means you should have to. As a go-getter mom, you will become efficient at delegating tasks. Whether you are at home or at work, you can assign tasks to those around you to take on some of the workload that is usually on your shoulders. You do not have to keep pushing yourself to the point of burnout just to get through your days. As you read through these methods, you will see that there are different solutions to the problems that you are facing. You have the power to make choices and still reach the same, or better, end results.

You are going to become an expert at so many different skills. As you read through this book, you will discover how to excel at the following:

- Finding and respecting your limits
- Figuring out your purpose at home and at work
- Making all of your goals and tasks happen efficiently
- Managing the goals that you are currently working toward
- Defining your own meaning of greatness to ensure realistic expectations
- Creating boundaries that you will successfully implement
- Clarifying your emotions and learning how to find great outlets for them

By using all of these resources, you will become even greater than you already are. Your kids will benefit because their mom will be refreshed and rejuvenated like never before. Those around you at work will also take notice because you will be readily available with new thoughts and ideas. Even your partner will see that they are so lucky to be with you because you have taken your life choices into your own hands; you hold all of your own power now.

You will no longer feel defeated by the roadblocks that try to get you down. Instead, you will see them as welcoming challenges that will test you and allow you to demonstrate your skills. There is nothing in life that you cannot handle, and this book will prove it to you by encouraging you to put yourself to work. When you have the motivation to be a great mom and a great career woman, it is going to show in everything that you do. Each action you take will be deliberate and purposeful.

As a mother myself, I understand the struggle. I thought I could only be one or the other: mother or career woman. I sacrificed my career for several years before realizing that I could have and do both. What I was most fearful of was losing precious time with my children. The years passed so quickly that I did not want to waste a second. What I learned was to take advantage of the downtime and really get to know myself. After figuring out what I truly wanted and needed to be happy, I figured out a way to make time for it all. I firmly believe that if something matters to you, then you will find a way to do the same.

Change can be scary, but change can also be wonderful. You will discover exactly what you need to do and how you need to apply each change. The great part is that you do not have to completely change every aspect of your life to be a great mom and an excellent employee. You can make small changes as needed, adjusting to the flow of the life that you are already living. When you do things this way, they feel less overwhelming. You will also be able to better track the progress you are making.

Get ready to begin your journey, and get excited. It is not only hard work that you have to look forward to in the future. While you excel at working hard, you also have many fun and exciting memories to look forward to and cherish. These are the moments that will keep you going and will keep your spirit uplifted. As you do your very best, even if you make mistakes along the way, never forget that you are a strong and empowered woman. You truly can do anything that you put your mind to if you try hard enough.

CHAPTER 1

You Can Do It All—Know Your Limits

You already know that you can do it all because this is probably what you are used to doing. A mother has countless tasks that do not end just because the day does. From the moment that you wake up until your head finally hits the pillow at night, you have an endless to-do list that is meant to serve your kids and deem you the "Best Mother" award that is such a well-deserved feat. What you do at work is very similar. You are always ready and willing to jump in when you are needed. The regular tasks that you take on are done with laser focus and commitment. You take your job seriously, and it definitely shows.

The credit that you get is far less than you deserve, but you humbly accept it and then do it all over again the following day. It is important to recognize that you are still an individual underneath each of these roles that you take on. You are your own person, and you are entitled to your own feelings and emotions. Just because you can do it all does not mean you should aim to do it all every single day. This is going to lead you straight to a point called burnout, and this can be very hard to recover from. Once you hit burnout, you feel like you have hit a wall.

When you have burnout, everything you do feels wrong. It is during these moments that you just can't seem to make your kids happy, and your boss is scolding you for forgetting to do something. This anxiety is enough to drive anyone to a point of burnout, but your new goal is to level out before you reach this point. You are going to make it a priority to recognize your own feelings as you are simultaneously taking on your two roles as mother and career woman. When you respect your feelings like you respect others' feelings, you will start to treat yourself better.

It can be hard to accept help, especially when you feel like you can handle everything if you just continue to push yourself further. This is going to test you and challenge you in new ways, but try your best to accept the help and to use the resources around you. This does not make you weak or any less of a mother or career woman. What this makes you is a savvy and efficient go-getter. When you can take from what is around you to alleviate your workload, you are doing what is best for yourself and for those around you.

How to Avoid Burnout

Burnout can happen to anyone at any moment, but hardworking mothers are especially prone. Though you are programmed to work hard and want to do it all, there might come a point where you are operating on fumes without even realizing it. Even the simplest tasks feel very hard to accomplish because you are so tired and worn down. This is a point that you will learn to avoid. By better managing your time and being mindful of your energy, you will be able to focus on what is most important to you. This will allow you to get everything done on your to-do list in a timely manner that aligns with your priorities. Your motherly duties and professional duties will both be fulfilled, and this will make everybody happy—yourself included.

Signs That You Have Burnout

Being able to recognize these signs will help you figure out what steps you must take next—these all fall in line with being burned out. Just because you are used to dealing with them does not mean that this is your default setting. You can make small changes to ensure that you can successfully manage everything in a stress-free way. Pay attention to these signs, and see how many you can identify with lately.

- **You Begin to Question Why You Do What You Do**

Your job used to bring you so much joy, but now it just makes you question what you are doing and why you spend so much time trying. A frustrating day at work can feel like you are wasting precious time that should be spent with your family. At the same time, you need to keep up all of the hard work to make a living and to excel in your field. It is truly not a good feeling to realize that your job no longer brings you joy, but the good thing is that this is usually temporary—burnout can make you feel like the joy will not return, but you need to realize that it will. By acknowledging that you are going through it, you can make changes to reduce your stress.

- **You Feel Like Time Is Running Out**

As a busy mother who also prioritizes work, you often feel like time is slipping through your fingertips. If you actually feel like time is being taken away from you, then this might be a sign that you are just burned out. There is never going to be as much time as you want because you will always find ways to fill every gap, but you need to work on prioritizing what is most valuable to you right now. Work with the time that you have, then focus on your most important duties. This is easier said than done, of course. This is why burnout is such a real possibility. When you feel this way, you might just want to give up or feel like you have to choose between the two. You *can* be a great mother and a great businesswoman, though. You just have to work on focusing on your priorities before the other tasks get the best of you.

- **You Always Feel Torn Between Two Roles**

The thing about you is that you take on many different roles. You should not feel like you have to choose just one! Burnout can trick you into thinking that you can only be a mom or that you can only be a career professional. If you are constantly feeling torn or like you are being spread too thin, then you might need to take a moment to regroup. This is just burnout talking, and it is trying to convince you that you cannot do everything that you set your mind on. The ultimate fact of the matter is that most people hold two or more roles in life—this is normal and accepted. You can do both without spreading yourself thin.

- **You Have Things in Life You Feel You Cannot Accomplish**

If you have ever stopped to think that you wish you could do something or experience something, then this is definitely a discouraging feeling. Your life seems like it has hit a point of no return, but this is untrue. You can still do everything that you have always wanted to do, including those goals that you had before you were a mother and even before you entered your field of work. The inspiration is quick to flee when burnout enters the picture. What you must do is work on finding a place for it in your life where it allows you to stay motivated and ambitious. You can accomplish new things, even if you have already been through many different life experiences and are established today.

- **You Frequently Wonder About Your Purpose**

Being a mother is a wonderful way to give your life a purpose. It is an automatic reason for you to wake up each morning wanting to better yourself. However, being a career professional can feel like an entirely different story. You might question what your purpose is at your current job and even wonder if you are truly as valuable as you think you are. Burnout will always push you toward the more natural option, which is your nurturing role. This is not to say that you must only pick one, though. You have a purpose in both of these worlds, despite what burnout wants you to think. It is your job now to figure out how to allow the two worlds to combine.

If you recognize yourself in any of these, then it is time to transform the way that you operate. Your day-to-day routine is going to change for the better, and you will be thankful that you no longer have to live with so much stress. By removing these harmful elements from your life, you will be able to pay attention to what matters most: your kids and your career.

Tips That Help

- **Find Harmony**

    Harmony is the art of combining two very different roles. You must learn how you can be a present mother while also giving work your all. It is possible, and all it takes is changing up the way that you spend the time you are given each day. Make the most of each workday, and then power down when you are off the clock. Focus on your family during this time. You need to separate your work self from your mom self. This is how you will eventually achieve a good balance that comes along with plenty of harmony.

- **Know Your Breaking Point**

    Before you break, you need to have an idea of what your breaking point is. If you do not know your limits, you will never be quite sure when you are about to reach them. To avoid burnout, you need to stop before you get to this point, not when you are already there. If you feel like you have reached your limit, then you have already exceeded it. Any move you make is going to feel like too much. Stop the problem before it starts—this is how you will achieve even greater results than you already do.

- **Fill Your Day With Joy**

    It's the little things that make your day so much better, and joy is definitely one of them. If you make it a point to fill each day with moments of joy, then you are less likely to reach a point of burnout. Having a short break at work and looking at some photos of your children can be all it takes to have those happy memories flooding back to your mind. See what you can do to make yourself feel good when you have free time. Even the smallest things will help you more than you think.

- **Schedule Free Time**

    Just as you schedule everything else in your life, you also need to make time for yourself! Free time needs to go on your schedule in some form. Even if you cannot block out a full hour of time for yourself, try to aim for even just 15 minutes. This time is going to make such a huge difference in your life, and it will give you something to look forward to that is stable and serene. Do not worry about increasing this time until you manage to get used to the 15 minutes. You can make it a goal to increase it slowly until you have the full hour or even more. Everyone has at least 15 minutes to spare each day. You just need to figure out where to fit yours in.

- **Change Your Environment**

    When you are finally able to get out of the environment that is causing you stress, even for only a short bit of time, this is going to help your brain reset. If you cannot just take a drive to the next town over to get things off your mind, you can take a break and take a walk around the room. It sounds funny, but this simple action can make a major difference in the way you are feeling. When you give yourself a simple change in scenery, you will start to let go of the stressors that try to latch onto you. This is going to protect you from burnout while also rejuvenating you a bit. While this is not a permanent solution to burnout, it will certainly help the situation from getting any worse.

- **Live Mindfully**

    Getting outside of your head is always recommended. When you cannot stop stressing over what is going on in your life, this might be a sign that you need to try and change your focus. Think about everything else that is going on around you. This is going to help you when you feel like you are sinking under all of your tasks and to-do lists. Being mindful is a great practice as a whole, and it will teach you that your situation is never as bad as it seems. Having this perspective is going to prevent you from panicking or trying to do too much at once. It serves as a reminder to be gentle to yourself and to observe what others are doing. You can learn many great coping skills when you just stop for a moment to observe.

Accepting Help

Plenty of people try to offer you help as a busy mom, your partner being one of them. Even though you know that this help would alleviate a lot of your stress, there still might be some type of thought in the back of your mind telling you that you need to take on all of these tasks on your own or else you are a failure. Not only is this untrue but it is going to take you one step closer to burnout. Acknowledge that everybody needs help sometimes—even the strongest people. This does not take away from how amazing you are at being a mother and an employee.

Get Rid of Perfectionism

When you feel the need to make everything in your life perfect, you are going to be met with disappointment. Nothing will live up to your expectations, and most of the things you do will feel like they are in vain. Teach yourself how to define your own "perfect." This means that you get to be in control of what is right and successful. You get to choose what ultimately works best for yourself, your family, and your career. This is a major secret to success, and many hardworking women who ditch the idea of perfectionism also feel a lot less stressed out on a daily basis.

You have likely been taught that perfectionism is the goal since you were younger. There has always been pressure in society for women to be the perfect wives, mothers, and career-oriented individuals. This is a lot to ask of one person, especially when asking them to do it without any flaws. Remember that you are only human—you are going to make mistakes! This is normal, and mistakes will teach you how to become even better. If you already know how to do everything, you will never reach the point of opportunity that offers you personal growth.

Ignoring the idea of perfection and focusing on your own personal goals will align you in a very positive way with what you truly want. This is going to keep you focused, and it will show you how you probably have countless resources around you that you are forgetting about. Never discount your partner—they want to help with the parenting! If you do have a special person in your life, chances are that they are more than ready to step in with the parenting duties. By sharing some of these tasks, you will not feel as overwhelmed when you do get the chance to spend some of your free time at home.

Think about the way that you interact with your peers. While you all have your own roles to play, you can still work together as a team to help each other out. With teamwork, the stress is spread to everyone instead of only landing on one person's back. Do not become the person that chooses to take on everything because you want to prove a point. Asking for help and delegating tasks at work is okay. It is not shameful and does not denote you as a failure. What it really means is that you are innovative and resourceful. You know how much you can handle, and it shows that you are willing to go the extra mile to get the job done in the most effective and professional way.

Once you can convince your ego to stay out of your way, your stress levels are going to decrease dramatically. Asking for help is not easy, especially when you are already used to doing something on your own. Just because you can does not mean that you should—this is a lesson that repeats. You will experience many moments where you think you might be able to push yourself to work just a few more hours a week or where you might be able to schedule just a few more activities for your children that you are responsible for. Think carefully about what you are doing to yourself and how you are managing your time. Asking for help is a sign of strength that shows you are on top of things!

Stop Worrying About What Others Think

There will be opinions sent your way through the rest of your entire life. People love to chime in and give you advice, even when this is the last thing you are looking for. Part of being a mother and career woman means knowing how to take certain advice to heart and how to take the rest with a grain of salt. The thing about advice is that it does not always have to be followed. It is merely a suggestion that you can listen to and then decide what to do with if you want to do anything with it at all. Never feel obligated to make any changes in your life just because someone steps forward with a false authority insisting that you should.

No matter what anyone else thinks about you or what you are doing, you still have a household to upkeep and a job to do. Your family and your career matter to you because they are two of the most important things in your life. The decisions that you make in relation to them must be made with proper care, and this does not always include taking outside advice. It does not matter how well someone knows you or how long they have been in your life. They are human, and they can still be wrong. Some people even choose to project advice that they wish they could follow onto others.

There might come a certain time when you do need advice, but you do not know how to ask for it. You might feel ashamed that you are at a loss, but it is nothing to feel bad about. Understanding that you do not have all the answers makes you humble, and there is a lot that you can learn from other people. Have a conversation with someone you trust if you feel that you do need some help by way of wise words. They should be able to guide you through the situation you are experiencing. Pick someone who is in a similar situation to you or has been there before—this is going to give you the best results because they can relate.

The thing about advice is that even good advice does not need to be followed exactly as given. Having a conversation with someone who can relate might inspire you to take a similar but different route. This will still be beneficial to you because it will give you that jump start you need to make a change. Life can be very difficult at times, but you always have caring people around you who want to see you succeed just as much as you do. Never take them for granted because, most of the time, they are always going to be willing to step in and offer up some of their wisdom from the life experiences they have been through.

Letting go of the thought that someone is judging your actions can be hard, even if it is someone you know means well. Human beings have the tendency to worry about someone else's opinions when other people are just worrying about the same thing. Let go of these fears by reminding yourself what you usually think about when you see a hardworking mother. You probably think to yourself that you admire her and that you respect her—this is also how people see you. Build yourself up, and make sure that your confidence is at its peak whenever you can. You deserve to feel just as strong as you truly are.

Acknowledge That You Are Still Strong

Your responsibilities might trick you into thinking that you are weak or that you cannot make everything happen in your life, but they are wrong. You are so strong! Believe in yourself as much as you believe in your children. When you can be kind to yourself this way, you will see that truly anything is possible. Even if you are asking someone for help around the house or with work, this does not negate the fact that you have worked so hard to get where you are and will continue to do so. You are going to get even stronger no matter what help you must request.

Listen to what your partner has to say to you. They are probably very encouraging and always willing to boost you up when you are in need. Your partner would not praise you if they did not mean it, so you should take these words to heart. Each time you are acknowledged for how great of a mother you are, how wonderful you are at keeping up with the household duties, and how you are an amazing partner, you need to believe this. It is through these compliments that you will build your self-esteem to become an even better version of yourself than you already are.

Consider that your friends and other loved ones also know you very well. They have seen you encounter many different situations that you have guided yourself through. You had to be innovative and come up with solutions to make everyone happy, even while sacrificing some of your own needs in the process. This takes so much strength, and it gets you to the point where you stand right now. It can always provide you with a nice boost of energy when you remember where you started. Think about how clueless you used to feel in the past when you first got the job or first became a mother. You learned along the way through firsthand experiences.

Look at yourself in the mirror each morning, and practice reciting positive affirmations to yourself. This is going to truly help you believe in how strong you are. It will also make you more open to receiving help from others because you will see that it is an asset rather than a weakness. By being willing to take on the extra hour of babysitting or by letting your co-worker assist you with your project, you are still making smart decisions that will get you one step closer to your goal of being a fantastic mother and excellent employee.

Helping others who are in need can also inspire you to accept help for yourself. When you have the means, do something for someone you care about. This is going to show you that it feels great to know that you can help out, and it will also make you realize that this is how others feel when they offer to help you. They are doing it out of the kindness of their own heart, not because they think you are weak and cannot do it alone. You have already proven that you are more than capable of being successful.

Remind yourself that you do not need to do it all! You can be wise by making the decision to delegate tasks when possible. Use these tips to your advantage, as they will all end up coming in handy. You can alternate between a few of them to determine which ones work best for you. Keep in mind that each mother is different. Based on your parenting style and how often you must be at work, you could potentially modify each of these tips to fit your lifestyle.

CHAPTER 2

Finding Your Purpose

Being a mother and an employee are two very essential parts of who you are, but these aspects do not complete your entire identity. Deep down, you have always been an individual. Before you became a mother and started on your current career path, you were a woman who had hopes, goals, and dreams. This person still resides underneath all of the new responsibilities and priorities that you must take on. One of the most important things you can do for yourself to encourage self-growth is to remind yourself of who you truly are. Finding your purpose can feel foreign these days, but you still have one.

You can actually have multiple aspirations, and it is not selfish if they do not all revolve around your kids or your work. By getting back in touch with who you truly are, you are going to see that you can create an action plan that satisfies your needs while also keeping up with your current responsibilities. Prioritizing yourself can be a very difficult decision to make when you are a hardworking mother, but it is something that can work for you. The first step begins by acknowledging that who you are deep down is important and that your needs matter just as much as anyone else's needs.

Any action that seems daunting will feel less stressful when you break it down into manageable steps. This is exactly what you can do when it comes to finding your true and current purpose in life. Do not think that you need to ponder over it for a few moments and have it all figured out—this process can take time, but you are going to be glad that you paid attention to it. By putting in this effort, you are making yourself an even better version of who you already are. It is empowering to know that you can still change your life while also keeping up with everything that is expected of you.

Steps You Can Take

No matter what stage of life you are in, it is never too late to better yourself. Finding your purpose makes you better because you are resetting your focus. You are acknowledging that there is more out there to accomplish and different ways to do it. Through your tenacity, you will become an even better mother and employee than you thought possible. Others are going to take notice of your newfound inspiration, and this should drive you to keep going and to strive for even more.

- **Donate Time, Money, or Talent**

When you do not know what to do with your own life, helping someone else's life can inspire you. By donating to a cause or an individual that you believe in, you are doing a good deed from the kindness of your heart. Many people who are charitable realize what matters to them through these actions. Think about the different causes that you can support and why your moral compass is pointing you in this direction.

You will end up learning a lot about yourself as you put some research into all of the different causes you are passionate about. Think about how you would like to change the world and who you can help through your actions. Even if you are not donating money, you can still donate your time and efforts. The talents that you have can come in handy in many ways that go beyond parenting and being a great employee.

Look into different types of volunteer work that you can complete during your free time. Not only are you helping others but you are making yourself feel useful. This is the epitome of living a purposeful life. When you can tell that your actions make a difference and that you matter in the world, you are going to feel rejuvenated and inspired to take creative liberty in your own life. You might feel like embarking on a new adventure or project.

Remember that you do not have to do the most to get the response that you seek. As long as you are being charitable with good intentions and out of the kindness of your heart, then you are going to be paid back in some way with something positive. Do not push yourself to volunteer five days a week when you barely have time to spend with your family after work. Be reasonable with your schedule. Just one day of volunteering is already better than none, so keep this in mind.

If you simply do not have time to donate to an organization right now, think about who you can help in your life currently. Being charitable to real people in your life will give you the same feeling of purpose and meaning. Just by doing something kind for someone in your life, you are going to realize that your actions could make their day. Depending on what you decide to do, they are going to feel something as a result of it.

Thinking about cause and effect can help you realize your true purpose. Every action that you take comes with an accompanying effect. The decisions that you come to are going to impact those around you, maybe even those you are unaware of. When you donate to causes and individuals you care about, you are living a more mindful life. This in itself is a very fulfilling purpose that will get you far in life. You will start to see that there is much more out there than your daily stressors and responsibilities. Joy can always be found if you cultivate it.

- **Listen to Feedback**

It can be difficult to define your passions, especially when you are already feeling stressed out by other aspects of your life. There are so many things that you probably enjoy doing on a day-to-day basis, but how are you certain if these are passions or simply hobbies that you enjoy? Most of the time, you never know until you pursue them. Listen to the feedback that you get from other people. When someone tells you that you are great at something or that they think you are talented, they are not saying this for personal gain—they believe in you, as you should believe in yourself!

You probably will not realize how important certain hobbies or passions are until they are brought to your attention. Think about what you spend most of your free time doing. When you are not working, taking care of your family, and taking care of yourself, what do you like to do for fun?

These are typically going to be your passions, and you will see that they are worth paying attention to because they can become a great way for you to unwind and better yourself.

If you are still not convinced, reach out to those who know you best. Your partner, loved ones, and best friends would likely be happy to give you some input. They will be able to determine what you are great at and why. This is sure to boost your overall confidence and remind you how you do have many great purposes in your life that do not solely revolve around your roles as a mother and a businesswoman. You can have passions that simply exist because you enjoy putting your time and effort into them.

Another way that you can define your passions is by asking those closest to you what reminds them of you. They will usually pick identifiers that you typically do or say, and this can lead you to discover what your current hobbies and passions are. When you like doing something, you are probably talking about it a lot more than you realize. Getting this other look at yourself can be very insightful and meaningful.

Look for patterns based on what you observe and what others say about you. Write down these observations as reminders of what you enjoy doing and what you stand for. This is going to help you solidify who you are as a person and what you are truly passionate about. This is what will give you more purpose, especially if you are feeling a little lost currently.

Whether others see you as the life of the party or a compassionate being, this is going to help guide you toward some new potential hobbies and passions that you can take on. The world is full of possibilities for you to take if you choose. This process should excite you and give you a sense of rejuvenation. Getting out of the old routine is really helpful, and it will show you that you are so much more than the labels you place on yourself.

- **Surround Yourself With Truly Positive People**

The people you spend the most time around are the ones who begin to influence you. Whether you realize it or not, you are influenced by the top five people you choose to spend your time with. This is a very powerful statement, as you might unknowingly be letting toxicity into your life just by who you hang out with or interact with. For example, if you are around people who do not have goals or motivation, this kind of behavior is going to rub off on you. It will make you start to feel the same way, even if you do have future plans for yourself.

You need to consider how much positivity you currently have in your life and how having even more of it will help you to find more of a purpose. If you let people into your life who have goals and are self-motivated, then this is going to inspire you. Living in a constant state of wanting to do more and to be more is healthy. It gives you just the right amount of drive to keep going with your own goals. This is not to say that you need to cut off all of your friends who are lazy or negative, but you just need to become aware of how much they are impacting you.

Take a social assessment. Think about those five people you spend the most time around or the most time conversing with. Consider what you talk about and what you do together. How do these actions make you feel? If the feeling is positive, then this is probably a great influence to have in your life. This is a person who will support your goals and make you feel like you have a purpose. The feeling that you are aiming for should be something that resembles inspiration or even pride in knowing that you are in great company.

If you think about someone and realize that they are always complaining or being negative, this is a red flag. Even if they are not being negative directly toward you, this is still negativity that you are allowing into your life. It is going to enter your mindset, and you might end up thinking the same way after too long. This is how you can lose all of your motivation in the blink of an eye, so you need to be really careful. Start to distance yourself from people like this to the best of your ability.

While it might not always be realistic to just stop conversing with someone or to stop seeing them around, you can still protect your energy in a way that shows them you are not going to be influenced by their behavior or what they choose to do in their own lives. Set a standard for yourself that you can maintain to make yourself rise above. You can do this without putting anyone else down in the process or without making anyone feel bad.

- **Start Conversations With New People**

Instead of burying yourself in your phone when you find yourself in new situations, try to look at your surroundings. Can you find any opportunities to converse with new people?

This can be very hard for most of us to do, especially in the digital age where we are more likely to send a friend request than to say hello to a stranger. This is how you meet new people, though. You might end up meeting more positive people you can have in your life that align with your values.

Do not be afraid to say hello to someone or to compliment something that you see about them that you like. This is not weird or awkward unless you make it feel that way. Build yourself up by realizing that you are a great and powerful individual with a lot of interesting traits and characteristics to offer in return. You can make new friends that might end up helping you to realize that there are certain passions you have always wanted to explore deep down inside.

Other people are able to ignite more purpose in your life because they give you new challenges. You need to learn about them and what they believe in. You need to assess your values and see if theirs matches your own. Getting to know new people is a great process that every hardworking mother should try to do at least every once in a while. It can be very hard to break free from your trusty routine, but you can do it. Believe that you are going to create great connections that will not only help you in life but provide you with even more confidants to listen to you.

Try to ask new people about any projects they are working on. This will sort of bypass the small talk that tends to stick around when you first meet someone new. When you start off with an interesting conversation, they will usually continue to be just as interesting. By showing them that you truly care about what they are working on, they are probably going to ask you about what you are currently working on. This is your chance to explain what you are passionate about and what gives your life meaning. Since this is a brand new person in your life, you will be able to go into full detail about it.

Not everyone is 100% comfortable with taking a social and extroverted approach, but you should try to push yourself outside of your comfort zone if the thought does scare you. This is how you are going to grow and learn more about yourself. If you only decide to stay in your routine and your social circle, you are closing off the energy that you are putting out into the world. By doing your best to challenge these norms, you are showing yourself that you can find new purposes and different meanings. This is going to be a great experience for you that will definitely lead to some exciting results.

- **Explore Your Interests**

This sounds like a rudimentary task, but there comes a point when you should explore your interests. You already know what you enjoy doing, but how do you know that you still enjoy doing these activities? Try to dig deeper. Define what you enjoy most and the feelings that these activities bring to your life. See if there are any other ways for you to make these things more prominent fixtures in your life by either making more time for them or expressing them in other ways.

For example, if you have a passion for creativity but have a very logical job, you can still express this passion from home. Use your creativity to make beautiful birthday party invitations or creative lunch ideas for the kids. You can do so much with what you are already passionate about if you just think about it from a different perspective. If work does not allow enough creative freedom, then your personal life certainly can.

This also presents you with a great bonding opportunity to share with your partner. If there is something you have been meaning to try or have always wanted to do, tell them! They might be on board to explore this activity with you, and this can allow you to grow even closer as a couple. Your entire life does not only need to revolve around you being a great mother and an excellent employee. While these are two aspects of who you are, these are not the only ways that you should define yourself. Try to see yourself for exactly who you are as a person in your entirety.

Think about what you do when you are on social media. You likely scroll through your news feed, "liking" photos that capture your attention. Why do you like these images? Is it because you wish that you could have the same in your life? If you do notice a pattern, take matters into your own hands—explore these things for yourself! See if you can manifest the same results in your life by taking a proactive approach. Liking a photo on social media can be enough to inspire you, but taking action will make it even more of a reality. You can achieve anything that you set your mind on.

You do not need to move to a rich neighborhood or buy a fancy car to feel fulfilled. You can do things realistically and on your own time. If you enjoy these luxurious things that you see on your news feed, you can set goals that will allow you to work hard until you have reached your own point of defined success. You get to say what is successful and what is not. Since this is ultimately up to you, it actually gives you a lot more power and freedom than you realize.

After you take inventory of the things that you have been liking on social media, take a look at what you portray. The way that you post says a lot about how you feel about yourself. See if you can align what you express to the world with how you feel about yourself as a person. This is going to ensure that you are being as genuine as possible, and it will keep you on track with your goals and dreams.

- **Consider Injustices That Bother You**

Injustices fuel you in the best way sometimes. While horrible things happen all around the world, you can use these causes to ignite that fire underneath yourself. See what is currently bothering you when it comes to world issues and injustices. This is going to give you a great reason to feel passionate about a cause and to even make a difference in what is going on. You might not think your voice or actions matter, but they truly do. Your intention of wanting to make something right that is wrong is already halfway toward making a difference.

Pick a cause that you believe in, and see what you can do to support it. Can you speak out on the issue? Using your voice and your platform is one of the most helpful ways to be useful when it comes to injustices that you cannot control. If there are any funding pages set up, you can make charitable donations to the cause to help make things right. You can also talk to your friends and loved ones about what is going on. Educating others on the cause is a very powerful way to help because too much misinformation can be spread so quickly.

If there is an opportunity for you to volunteer in person that relates to the injustice you are passionate about, take it! This is going to be very fulfilling, and it will give you a chance to see that you can do big things in your life. This provides you with the ultimate purpose and the great feeling of knowing that you are actually making a difference with something that you care a great deal about. No matter what you choose, you can always do more than what you are doing right now. Do some research, and you will see the countless options.

Keep in mind that advocating for injustices can be very draining. This is not going to become your main purpose but a purpose that you keep on the side for when you have time. Some people will make the mistake of championing for a cause until it takes over their entire life—you do not have time to do this. You are already a supermom and an important fixture at your job, but you can devote your free time to learning about the cause and spreading awareness so that others will also feel inspired to help.

You must also remember that not everybody is going to share the same passionate views that you have. You will not be able to change everyone's mind, but that is not your job. As long as you are advocating for a cause you believe in and doing so in a way that is fair, then what other people think of you will not matter. You can keep doing what you want to do and helping the cause in the way that you see is best. Remember that you do not always have to donate your money to make a difference. Your time is just as valuable.

- **Discover More of What You Love**

On the opposite end of the spectrum, you already have a great list of things that you enjoy doing in life. Think about all of these things and why you love them so much. You are going to expand on these activities and passions in a way that will make you feel even more involved and fulfilled by having them in your life. This can ultimately lead you to find new purposes that were just beneath the surface this entire time.

Pick one passion each day, and see what you can do to enhance it. If you love watching a reality show that is about dancing, have you ever considered taking a dance class yourself? This idea might sound outlandish at first, but it can ignite a spark inside that you did not realize was present. You will never know until you try, so you might as well give it a try before you completely write off any new idea. See if you can expand on your current passions in this way by making them even more prominent in your life.

Anything that you deem fun and worth your time is something that you can absolutely become passionate about. This can range from activities to getting involved with certain people or groups. Do not settle yourself short in fear of judgment. Nobody who judges you wanting to live a more inspired life deserves to be close to you. This is not going to be a person who supports you and uplifts you when you need it most. Keep this in mind if you are fearful of what others around you will think as you pursue new passions.

As you consider what you are already passionate about, think about how loving these things has enhanced your own skills. What traits do you bring to the table? What can you say with confidence that you are great at? Work on this exercise by writing down everything you can think of. Keep adding to this list, and make sure that it is visible all the time to serve as a reminder that you have so much untapped potential in life. You have already made it this far, so who is to say that this is the end? There is a lot more out there for you.

Being a mom and a businesswoman does not signify the end of a chapter in your life. This is only one element of who you are and what you stand for. There is so much more to you that you can discover and so many other chapters for you to read about yourself. Get to know yourself on an even deeper level, and try to remain free of judgment. You already know that you are trying your best to be a great mom and employee, so you are going to exert this same energy toward any other passions you discover.

Keep in mind that there is no deadline by which you should complete these steps. You need to try and do what feels right and what you realistically have time for. Never push yourself to make any changes that feel unnatural or else you are just going to rebel against them. Finding your purpose should be an eye-opening and fun experience—nothing that adds stress to your already full plate.

CHAPTER 3

Making It Happen

Your dreams will come true: Repeat this until you truly start to believe it. No, it will not simply happen by chance or being in the right place at the right time. Achieving your dreams comes with commitment and a lot of hard work. You must be ready and willing to put in the time and energy that it takes to succeed, but you can channel all of the hard work that you have already accomplished to get there. What you need now is an action plan that is suitable for your current lifestyle. This plan is going to get you one step closer to completing your goals while still keeping your priorities straight. You will not have to sacrifice being a great mother or being a hardworking employee in the process.

The only person that can make this happen is you and comes with both power and pressure. Try not to let the thought overwhelm you because it is one of the few things in life that you do have control of. You get to decide how much effort you put into making your dreams come true, and the results will reflect this. Depending on what you do and how you try to do it, you will see your life begin to transform before your eyes. It is truly magical when you realize that you have everything you have ever wanted for yourself, and it is all thanks to your tenacity.

Always give yourself credit when it is due—this will keep you feeling proud of yourself! You deserve a pat on the back for how far you have already come. Now, it is time to put the effort into turbo drive. You are going to think strategically to come up with an action plan that makes sense to you. It will focus on enhancing your current strengths and building up your weaknesses so that you can turn them into new strengths. No matter how you approach this endeavor, it is going to be an exciting time in your life as both a mother and an employee.

When creating this plan, make sure you are doing it for the right reasons. You should want to achieve your goals because they matter to you, not because someone is expecting you to act this way or to be a certain way. Take into account that you are an individual who has freedom and independence. You get to decide what matters most and what you are going to do about it. You can either remain stagnant where nothing will change, or you can tackle this head-on to make a big effort at making all of your hopes and dreams a reality.

Creating Your Action Plan

As you begin the process of creating your action plan, it is important to understand all of its components. In this plan, you will include a detailed description of what you would like to achieve, the steps that must be taken to get to the end result, resources that you can use to help you along the way, deadlines, and ways to evaluate your progress. It sounds simple on paper, but you know that it is going to involve a lot of planning and following through. After this plan has been implemented, it is up to you to make progress on it. You need to commit yourself to this plan and to the deadline that you set for yourself.

The good thing is that this does not have to be an overwhelming process. Any great plan is carefully crafted to ensure that there are no loose ends. By the end of its creation, you should have a very clear idea of what you hope to achieve and how you will get there. This will actually bring you more peace of mind and a newfound sense of inspiration that will carry you through life.

Step 1: Define the End Goal

You need to be crystal clear about what your end goal is. You cannot simply list "success" or "accomplishments" as the end goal. That is too much of an open-ended option, and you will definitely stray from this task when you leave it this vague. Think hard about what you would like to work on right now, and try to detail this with as many words as possible. Write it down on paper so you can see it before you. Maybe you want to earn that promotion so you can have a nicer office, or maybe you are interested in becoming the head of the PTA at your child's school so you can become more involved in their education. Perhaps the goal is entirely personal. You might just want to become a more compassionate individual so you can easily understand those who come to you with hardships.

No matter what you choose, make sure to be as specific as possible. Think about what accomplishing this goal will do for your life and how it will benefit you. To help you even further, you can use this acronym for setting SMART goals during the first step:

S: Specific—Set a goal that is clear and defined.

M: Measurable—Pick something that allows you to track your progress.

A: Attainable—Be realistic about what you are trying to accomplish.

R: Relevant—Make sure it aligns with your values and beliefs.

T: Time-Bound—Set a reasonable deadline for yourself to keep you on track.

When you set SMART goals, you are going to be a lot more organized during the creation of your action plan. After you have this objective written down, run it through the SMART goals one more time to make sure that it all aligns with this acronym. If there is anything missing, see if you can alter it so that it is more specific and intentional.

This is a great way to set goals for not only the present but also in the future. When you think about any other goals that you want to set from either work or at home, you can go through these SMART goals to make sure that you are not setting yourself up for failure. Many people are too vague or unrealistic with their goals, and this will lead to inevitable disappointment that causes them to give up. This will not be you. Now that you understand exactly how to set your goals, you are going to thrive.

Take a look at what you have ended up writing down, and see how it makes you feel. This goal should make you feel excited, like you are about to take on a whole new project. It should not feel stressful or daunting. Try to view this as something positive that is going to truly change your life for the better. If anything about it starts to stress you out, take a few deep breaths while remembering that nothing is going to change overnight. You are still creating your action plan.

Step 2: List the Steps

The next thing you must do is create steps that you will follow; you have a starting point and an end goal, but what goes in between? These steps are going to fill in the blanks for you. They will guide you through the process and teach you how to get there. It can be difficult when you have no idea how to get from point A to point B but do not let this discourage you. Nobody has it all figured out right away. If they did, then everyone would already have all of their goals completed. You are still learning, and you are willing to learn to make this massive improvement to your life which says a lot about you.

If you are trying to become a more compassionate person, think about what makes someone compassionate to begin with. What are the traits that they would possess? This part will have you do some research no matter what your goal is. Once you figure this out, you can then begin to think about how to obtain these traits for yourself. You might already have some of them. In this case, you would think about how to further enhance them. When you find out some concrete steps you can take, you will list them as steps to get you closer to your goal. Keep double-checking that each step you write down directly and clearly aligns with your end result.

While this is only one example, you will treat any goal that you have in the same way. Break it down into steps that are manageable and realistic. If you need some extra inspiration, do some research on others that you feel possess the end result you want. Reading the success stories of others can be a great way to inspire you to do better and will also give you some ideas of what steps you can take for your own action plan. Read about people you admire, and try to grasp onto some bits of inspiration as you do this. You can be inspired by those in your life and strangers you have never met before. Do not rule anyone out as you are thinking about who possesses the qualities that you seek.

If it is possible, have a conversation with someone who has what you want. Talk to them about their journey and their struggles. Listen to their experience, as it can become very valuable to you later on. When you start going through the same motions, you might be able to learn from what others have already done. If you are close to this person, they might also be willing to share some tips and tricks with you. In a way, you are accepting a mentor in your life. No matter how successful you are on your own, it is always a positive thing when you can have someone else who is successful in your life to act as a mentor who is willing to guide you.

Step 3: Prioritize Tasks and Add Deadlines

Once you have everything planned out, the organization process will begin! It is time to set your priorities straight. By taking a look at all of the steps that you have written down, you now need to determine which steps are most important. This can be difficult because you might feel like they are all of equal importance. Think about this in the way of time and how much time you have to complete each step. Some of them might be time-sensitive steps. By default, these steps are going to move higher up on your list of priorities. It helps to put stars by the tasks that are deemed most important to complete. Once you have everything separated like this, try to write down all of the steps again in order from most to least important.

Keep reordering the steps until you feel that you have a list that makes sense to you. It is okay if you feel the need to sleep on it and to come back to it with fresh eyes. This is for your benefit, so you need to make sure that the process works for you. During this stage, you do not really need to take others into consideration because this is your goal to achieve. You are setting out to do something great for yourself and to enhance your life. Do not settle for a list of tasks that do not make sense to you or that are based on what others want you to do.

After you have the final list written down, create a deadline for each task. It can be a foreign feeling when you are the one assigning all of the deadlines. You might not know how hard to be on yourself because you want a challenge but do not want unnecessary added stress in your life. Set realistic deadlines that you know you can achieve, but try not to make them too easy. For example, giving yourself two weeks to do each one is a little too lax. This will make your end result seem very far out of reach. Try to go with your instinct and then subtract a few days from this. By doing so, you are going to challenge yourself while still setting realistic goals that you know you can accomplish.

You do need to consider what you already have on your plate. Between family life and work, you already have a massive to-do list that can seem like it never ends. Now, you are adding even more steps to this list, but this does not have to be a bad thing. Since you are creating this from the ground up, you know how much you can handle. You should be able to form a realistic schedule for yourself that you can fit in between what you are already doing. These deadlines can be adjusted if necessary—this is a big benefit that you have at your disposal.

Step 4: Set Milestones

Milestones are similar to goals in the sense that they will keep you on track. You can create these milestones to give yourself certain points to reach as you make progress along the way. When you have them in place, they will keep you motivated because it will not seem like you have to wait as long until you are rewarded with the feeling of accomplishment. They will also give you something to truly look forward to as you start your day—more of a structured approach to taking on your goal.

To set your milestones, start from the end goal and then work your way back. This strategy helps because it will teach you what must be done right before you reach the goal. You can work off this information by creating evenly spaced milestones from there until you are at the beginning. Consistency is everything when you are using milestones to help keep you motivated. Make sure that they are just as attainable as your end goal. You want to ensure that you are not setting yourself up for disappointment with these milestones.

If you are still unsure of how long to set your milestones for, aim for two weeks in between each one. This gives you enough time to spend actively working on the process yet also allows you to know that you are close to an achievement. You will learn a lot about your work ethic when you include milestones in your action plan because this presents you with even more challenges to face. You are going to tackle them head-on and with ease.

Milestones can prevent your goal from getting boring. When the steps start to feel too mundane, knowing that you are reaching milestones can really help you keep the entire plan more exciting. Nobody likes to work hard without any recognition, so you must give this to yourself. Acknowledge your successes by praising yourself when you can. You deserve to feel happy about what you are doing, and you do not need to wait for anyone in an authoritative position to tell you otherwise. You are strong enough on your own, and your self-esteem is going to thrive once you figure out that you can fulfill these needs without waiting on someone else.

As you look back on your work, you will see how much milestones helped you reach the end goal. You can implement this same process again for the next goal that you focus on. This process is going to happen multiple times in your life, as action plans are useful for many different occasions and at many different times. Do not consider this a one-time method for being productive or for staying motivated—you will learn that creating an action plan that has milestones will become one of your go-to techniques for when you are working hard on something you care about.

Step 5: Identify Resources Needed

With any goal, you are going to need resources to implement the plan. Step five encourages you to think about all of the resources you anticipate needing before you begin. You might not know what all of them are right away, but you can prepare by having the ones that you are aware of from the start. This is going to keep you organized and on track. By having everything you need at the ready, you will be able to gracefully handle any roadblocks that try to stand in your way.

If you can already identify that there are some resources you do not have, then you are giving yourself a prime opportunity to get them in place for yourself before you begin. Think about what you plan on doing ahead of time to make the process even easier. You might need to get into contact with helpful individuals or those who have something that you can use to assist you with your plan. Maybe you need to create these connections because you are going to need them later on. No matter what the case is, try to always think a few steps ahead of the plan.

Another resource that you need to plan for is financing. Will your end goal require a budget of any sort? This is definitely something for you to consider before you begin and work on figuring out how you will afford any of the resources that might cost you money. Those who do not think about a budget are often left stopped in their tracks during their action plan because they did not account for the expenses. Not all plans and goals require spending money, but you need to make sure that if yours does, you will have all of the funding available before you begin.

Think about any fundraising opportunities you can achieve before you start your action plan. There are likely many other people who also believe in your cause, and you can use their help with funding if you can make a great pitch. When making a pitch, you will want it to sound appealing to all involved. Come from your heart, and tell them why this cause matters to you and why you believe that they should help out. You would be surprised at who is willing to help when you simply ask.

If you do not have any costs that are assigned to each task, then you can skip the fundraising step for now. Do not completely write it off, though. You never know if you might need money in the future to keep your goal growing healthy and strong. Always think about the future and what might happen. A goal does not end once you reach it; this is simply the beginning of something new for you.

Step 6: Visualize Your Plan

Visualization is a great technique to use for any goal. When you do this, all you are doing is thinking about what your life is going to be like once you achieve the plan. Consider all of the benefits you will now have access to once you have your end result before you. Think about how this will make you feel and what difference it will make in your life. Will you be proud of yourself? Will others recognize you for your successes? So much can change based on one small decision that you decide to make for your life.

As you visualize the plan, try to put it in simple terms. This means that you should be able to explain your vision to anyone, and they will be able to understand it. Practice talking about your action plan with people in your life that you trust. Make sure that they support you and what you are doing. This is going to give you a boost of confidence and remind you how you can do anything you set your mind to. You can visualize the plan in your head at first, but try to bring it to life by writing it down on a vision board of sorts.

You can use a flowchart, a branching effect, or even simple color coding to convey your message. Do not forget that you can also use imagery to enforce your point. By looking at images of your end goal, this will keep you motivated and striving for success. You might feel like there is a fire lit beneath your feet that is reminding you to keep moving and to keep going. Include all of the elements of your plan, from the end goal to the smaller steps that come in between. You need to make sure that they are all there on your vision board so that you do not forget anything.

Imagine that you are an outsider who does not know anything about this plan or the goal. Would the board make sense to you? This is a good way to see if you are missing anything and how you can fill in these gaps. Work on your board on a regular basis to keep the ideas fresh in your mind. You might even come up with some new ones along the way. Creativity is always the beginning of something great when it comes to creating an action plan. With your creativity, you will see that new solutions seem to be more readily available than they once were. Accept feedback from those you show your vision board to. This is not something that you need to take personally or to feel offended by. If your vision does not make sense to someone, ask them why and then you can see what to improve.

Step 7: Evaluate and Update

Now, you are ready to begin the plan. Execute it with confidence and grace. You have everything that you need to proceed, and all it takes is the determination to make it a regular part of your life. As you go, try not to get too lost in the plan. You need to always be monitoring your progress and assessing your accomplishments. This is what the tasks and milestones are for. When you can take a look back at all that you have done, you will see how far you have come from where you started. Journaling can help you with this. Write about how you feel about the plan each day.

You will notice that the more time passes, the more confident you will grow. The plan is going to become second nature to you, and it will likely become something exciting that you feel like working on. It can be a daunting task in the beginning, but new things usually are a scary adventure. You will get used to this, just like you mastered being a great mother and employee. Treat this as you would either of your other roles. You can be masterful, hardworking, and driven. This is not a plan that you are going to forget about in a week—commit to it.

Each time that you complete a task or reach a milestone, put a checkmark next to it. This is a very simple step, but it is going to make you feel very accomplished when you can see what you are actually doing. Visual cues help tremendously because they serve as reminders that you are truly making progress. When you are feeling down about the process or thinking that you are not doing enough, just take a look at all of the checkmarks you have listed so far. This will help you and motivate you to keep checking more things off the list.

Another benefit of monitoring your progress is giving yourself a chance to see anything that is pending or delayed—this is bound to happen because you are already living a busy life. This is not something you should feel bad about, but it can show you where you might need to regroup and work harder. Being a hardworking mom also means being accountable for your actions. If you can see that you are slipping up with the plan, then you can also fix it.

These are all the steps necessary to follow if you are ready to create your action plan. Do this now because there will never be a "perfect" or "better" time to do so. If your end goal is something that you truly want, you will make time for it in any way that you can. Plan carefully, and go through all of the steps with purpose. You are going to make big things happen in your life—bigger than the things you have already accomplished before.

CHAPTER 4

Managing Your Goals

Every hardworking mother has goals, but how are they defined? Typically, a goal is either going to pertain to the job that you have or your personal life. With all of the different kinds of goals that you might want to create action plans for, it can get a little tricky when it comes to prioritization. In this chapter, you will get to learn the difference between the two and how to better manage them. Just because you have one set of goals does not mean you cannot have another. With both in your life, you will learn how to create a balance that works well for you.

Goal setting is a super important part of life. Even if you are the type of mother who goes with the flow, having goals will keep you organized and motivated. You can still be the same free spirit with goals in your life. They teach you that your hard work pays off and that you can still accomplish even more for yourself than you already have. At work, having professional goals keeps the job interesting. It shows you that you do not have to get stuck in a mundane routine that feels dated.

As you reach certain milestones in life, your goals are bound to change and grow with you. What you wanted before you became a mother might not be the same as what you want now—this is okay! Goal setting and management are two very personal practices that you will learn how to master.

Let your goals change. Strive for the things that you deem important and that matter most to you. This is why they are your goals and not anyone else's aspirations.

Personal vs. Professional

Personal Goals: What Are They?

Your personal goals typically revolve around your happiness, well-being, and family life. They do not always have to include other people, as it is healthy to have goals that only pertain to yourself. These are the goals that most individuals have, the things that they wish they could accomplish or want to do in life. They can range from losing weight to saving up enough funds to buy a new wardrobe. There is no right or wrong when it comes to personal goals because they are so individualized. If you want something and are willing to work hard for it, then it should go on your list! Get used to the idea that you can want something that only benefits you. This is not selfish, as it is actually a form of self-care.

Personal goals will typically revolve around your current feelings. This is why they can change so rapidly. Even the things that you wanted a year ago might differ from what you currently want. Make sure that you are in touch with your emotions because you might end up heading in a direction you are unsure of. For example, if you are feeling down about yourself lately for any reason, this can hinder the way that you plan out your personal goals. Your self-worth might be in question, and your value as a person will feel very low. This is why it is essential to make sure you are in touch with your emotions and able to process them before you create your list of goals. Make sure that each one is benefitting you in some way.

If you do not feel good about something in your life, you have the ability to change this through your personal goal setting. Make it your passion to fix all that bothers you about your life and the people in it. While you cannot fix everything through setting goals, you can make a pretty large impact on your situation. This is how you get out of the self-imposed rut that most people create for themselves. It tends to happen to the hardest working mothers, but it is not a place you need to stay for long. Once you recognize that you are there, you can make a change for the better.

In some ways, personal goals can feel harder to achieve than professional ones. These goals are the ones that you need to go out of your way to make time for. With the latter, you are already working and on a career path, so they often blend in with your current tasks. Personal goals do need to be taken just as seriously. This is why you need to create self-imposed deadlines to keep that slight pressure on. If you are too lax about them, you will never accomplish them because they will not feel important. Show yourself that you deserve all of these things that you want and that you *will* make them happen.

When you live your life without personal goals, you are simply going through your routine. This can feel very positive and look very positive, but there is not much substance to it. With personal goals, you have more potential for personal growth. Everything that you are right now will be intensified through your achievements. What you stand for will be even stronger and better than it is right now. You should want to achieve more personal growth in life because this will make you a better person in every aspect.

You will notice that a lot of unhappiness stems from not having any motivation. Without personal goals, you are simply existing on others' time. You feel like you do not get to decide much in your life, and this can lead to a feeling of entrapment. This is the feeling that you want to avoid at all costs, the one that causes you to believe that you are a failure in some way. Your inner critic can be super tough on you if you let it, but this does not have to happen to you. With the strength that you already have, you can rise above it—tell it that you are worth more than this.

Begin thinking about what you want in your life right now. This does not have to be an immediate or rushed process. It is better to take your time with it and to ensure that you are really prioritizing your own needs for once. As a mother, there are seldom times when you actually put yourself first. With your personal goals, this is your chance—they are all about you. While they will indirectly impact those around you, these goals shape you as a person and give you what you need to feel happy in life.

When you think about something that you want, jot it down. Make a draft of a list that you can return to and organize later. Sometimes, inspiration will hit at inconvenient times. Since you are such a busy person, you cannot always sit down and write them all out at once. Give yourself enough time to truly consider everything and anything that your heart desires. Organize your list, and feel proud of yourself as you do this. What this means is you are taking a step in the right direction; you are taking a step toward personal growth and becoming the true go-getter that you know you are.

Professional Goals: What Are They?

Your professional goals are your aspirations. They are usually more long term than your personal goals because they take more steps to complete. Professional goals can often seem more daunting because they depend on other people to complete them. You might seek a promotion or a new job, but you cannot always just walk into the office and get exactly what you want. You will need to work hard, prove to your superiors that you are the right person for the job, and then earn your spot. Professional goals are challenging, and they can often lead to stress for busy mothers who already have a lot to think about.

The great thing is that you will learn how to manage both sets of goals at once. You can have personal goals and professional goals at the same time while working on them simultaneously. You have probably been told before that you cannot do both because you are a mother. Your children can still be your priority while you work on yourself—this is possible with the right time management skills! Do not let anyone allow you to think that this is an impossible task. You are going to succeed and give yourself the confidence necessary to do so.

As you know, you get to define your own version of success. You need to set the parameters for what successful behavior is in your eyes. This is going to guide you as you work on setting and completing professional goals. You will see that once you do this, the pressures of the outside world will not be as prominent any longer. This will take away a lot of stress. Success can be anything that you make it—this is what makes you feel proud of yourself, accomplished, and closer to your goals. You are in control when it comes to this definition, and that is something to be proud of.

There are going to be lots of suggestions thrown your way when it comes to success and how to define it. Your peers are going to offer these suggestions in a helpful way, but they will not always be right. These paths might be acceptable for them, but they might not be the ones that you want to take—this is okay. Learn how to talk about others' goals and aspirations without completely changing your own. You can gain inspiration from others, but you do not have to mimic their plans entirely. Stick to what you truly want and what you know you can do. Challenge yourself in a way that benefits you and gets you closer to finishing the next item on your to-do list.

Most of the time, your professional goals are going to be timed in a strict manner. This is because you cannot control most of these aspects. You need to work around the schedules of others and the influences that are external. Being a working professional means learning how to go with the flow, even despite what you want for yourself. You cannot simply rely on your emotions and passion to get you through these goals. While this is a part of completing them, you must also lean on logic to get by. You will learn this as you create more professional goals for yourself. See if you can challenge the negative voices in your head that try to say you cannot do it.

This tends to happen because of societal pressures. Society wants you to believe that you can only fit a certain role and never grow beyond it, but you definitely can. You can become an even greater mother and career woman while checking the tasks off your to-do list. You know what you are capable of, and now, it is time to show the world. Understand that it is up to you to allow yourself to shine. There will not always be a clear opportunity for you to leave your mark, so you need to make your presence known. Show others why you should be valued and treated with respect.

This all starts from within. Once you can value yourself, you will be able to convince others that you are valid and worthwhile. Think about all of the professional goals that you have accomplished thus far—this is amazing! You are doing such a great job, and you can keep this momentum going. As long as you keep yourself busy, these goals are going to keep you motivated. There might be a little stress and pressure involved but only in the best way. This will be enough to light that fire underneath you. It will teach you how to manage stress and turn it into drive instead.

The great thing about the timetable surrounding professional goals is that you do have some control over it. You know what a realistic deadline is given your other tasks and responsibilities. You can set your goals to work around these tasks and to ensure that you are able to complete everything. Teach yourself that you can be disciplined enough to stick to all of your responsibilities while also striving for more. It does not have to stop just because you feel successful right now; the success can continue to grow if you are willing to work hard at it.

Money does not equal happiness, but it is a contributing factor. When you have enough money to care for yourself and for your family, this is a big feeling of success and accomplishment. You do not need an abundance of money to feel like you are doing well in your life, but knowing that you can earn enough to take care of your family and your needs will go a long way for your mental health. Try to have some monetary goals in mind, even if you are not very financially driven. This is going to push you even further, encouraging you to keep going.

When you are successful professionally, this is going to create a ripple effect in other aspects of your life. Once you start accomplishing these goals, you are going to have more confidence to accomplish your personal goals. They all go hand in hand, and this is why it is so important to keep both in your life at the same time. Challenge yourself by always keeping yourself busy with goals and tasks. This is going to benefit your personal growth and your ability to keep pushing through even the toughest times. You can do anything that you set your mind to, as long as you are willing to prove it to yourself.

How to Focus On All Your Goals

Now you have your goals in place. You know the steps that you need to take to get there, but what comes next? You must implement all of your actions and make intentional decisions that will allow you to achieve them. This requires focus and patience. With all that you have going on in your life, this can be tricky. The tips below are going to help you concentrate. They will remind you of what is truly important and why you should be focused on all of your goals at all times.

Set the Focus On You

It is easy to assign your personal goals to another individual who can help you make them come true, but this is not necessary. You can make them happen all on your own by setting the focus on you. Try not to delegate tasks while working on your personal goals. Think about how you can complete all of these actions on your own. While using all your resources, think about how you can still hold yourself accountable for what is happening and what progress you are making. This is how you will achieve personal growth.

Setting the focus on yourself is not selfish. They are personal goals for a reason, and you deserve the attention you can give to yourself. Think of this as a way that you are going to make yourself even better as a mother and an employee. You do need this time for yourself, just as you often need alone time to relax. It is what you deserve, and you do not have to feel guilty for wanting this kind of element in your life. Every hardworking mother deserves to feel this way and deserves to feel confident in all that they have accomplished so far. The best is yet to come with your goals.

Creating a personal bucket list can help you when it comes to checking personal goals off your list. This makes the process entirely about you and also makes it seem more fun and exciting. A bucket list can include any personal goals that you have, both long term and short term. It will be a list that is filled with things that almost feel impossible, but you are going to prove yourself wrong as you complete them. Show yourself that you are capable of doing anything. These bucket list goals will stay with you for life, and you can continue adding to the list even as you check off new goals.

Tell other people in your life about your goals! This is a great way to celebrate them and make them feel even more real. Once you tell someone about what you are striving toward, it makes the whole process seem tangible. Tell your best friend and your loved ones. Explain your progress and your end goal. Show them that you are willing to work hard for what you believe in. This is going to encourage you to keep going, and it is going to build up a wonderful support system around you.

Understand the Timeline

When you create your deadlines, you need to make sure that they make sense given your current lifestyle. You cannot expect yourself to meet your goals and to reach deadlines when you only give yourself minimal time to get there. Be realistic with time because you know how precious it is. There are many other things that you need to share your time and energy with, but your goals will become one of these things. Careful planning is a necessity, and understanding your personal timeline is the key to creating a list of goals that are actually going to be attainable.

If you know that it is going to take you a little bit of extra time to work on a goal, give yourself this time! There is no rule that says you have to rush through everything, especially when you want to give it your all. You can still challenge yourself in a way that creates motivation without adding any additional stress to your plate. Your goal should be to make yourself feel excited to work on these goals, not dreading the thought of the tasks. Teach yourself that you are in control of the time management: You get to decide what you do with your extra and available time.

Plan for the unexpected. You never know when something is going to come up that will interfere with your goals, but that is okay—you can work around these little moments and still get everything done. There might be delays in your plans, but you will not feel as hindered if you are expecting this to happen. You basically have to convince yourself to be okay with the unexpected, never truly knowing what to anticipate. This is what makes being a hardworking mom so fun and exciting. You have all of these goals in mind, but things are not always going to go perfectly according to plan.

Some goals are not going to be as dependent on deadlines as others, but this does not mean they should be bumped lower on your list of priorities if they matter to you. This is all about personal preference, and you get to decide which ones you focus on and which ones can wait. You will learn how to manage them all the more that you practice making an effort to complete them on a daily basis.

Make Them Measurable

There are some goals that are easy to measure. For example, if you have a goal to save up $500, this is going to be very easy to keep track of. You will be able to see the results of real-time growth in your savings account. Other goals might not be this simple. You need to figure out how to make all of your goals measurable in some way so that you can refer back to these milestones. They will guide you and push you to keep going strong. Make sure that you consider all of the steps that you have laid out for yourself and the milestones that you have in mind—these will both help you when measuring your progress.

If you cannot measure the goal itself, then see if you can measure the way you feel about the goal. Once you start to make progress, it should feel more realistic to you. What once seemed impossible will now be completely plausible. You will also notice that you have more time, energy, and motivation to devote to the cause. That is an improvement that you can definitely measure, and you should truly feel proud of yourself for doing so. It is not easy to get past the first few days of trying out something new.

As you are measuring your goals, try to avoid the terms "better" or "more." You need to appreciate the effort that you are putting into them as you work hard on them. There is always going to be some type of room for improvement, but using such definitive words only adds unnecessary pressure to the process. Be kind to yourself, and appreciate what you have done so far. The best is yet to come, and once it does, you can start again with some brand new goals! This is when goal setting becomes even more fun.

The more that you can build yourself up, the better you will feel when you make accomplishments. Try to use positive affirmations at all times. Tell yourself that you are doing a fantastic job, and you are doing the best you can. The more you get into this habit, the more you will start to believe these words. Understand that nobody else can tell you how well you are doing on your own goals. The process is entirely personal and up to you.

Define Your Own Goals

You are going to be influenced by many people around you at all times. Your peers, friends, and even your partner might have their own personal and professional goals that you could feel pressured to mirror. The great news is that this is not necessary. Your goals are your own, and that is what makes them special! You ultimately get to decide what you want to do and how you would like to define your goals. Try not to let any type of peer pressure get into your head, even the kind that seems positive at first glance. You are an individual, and you can decide what you want and need to be happy.

If you ever take a look at social media, you are going to see plenty of different goals and aspirations, but think about if they fall in line with what you actually want. Many influencers get paid to promote certain products and lifestyles on your timeline for the purpose of trying to get you involved in the same activities. From the clothes they wear to the food they eat, you might find yourself copying these behaviors and striving for these goals even though they are not your own. Think about how you use social media and if it is healthy for your mindset.

It can be a great way to kill time, but it can also be a great way to kill your inspiration. You might find yourself willing to settle for less than you deserve when you are just copying what other people say and do. Always set your focus on yourself, and you will be on the right path. You can consider how your actions will affect your family and loved ones but, above all, think about how they will make you feel. You should be proud of yourself once you complete a goal. There should be a true sense of accomplishment present with each item you check off your to-do list.

Instead of using social media as a way to gather ideas, you can use it to celebrate your own accomplishments. Post what you are proud of and what makes you happy. This kind of energy is infectious, and it will encourage you to do exactly what you want in your life. You might even inspire those who follow you to do the same. There is no sense in banishing the platforms if they bring you joy, but you must determine if they do or don't first.

With these tips in mind, you can complete all of your goals, both personal and professional. You can do anything that you are willing to work hard to do, and this is something that you have proven to yourself time and time again. Do not let anyone underestimate your abilities or doubt you because you are the one who is in charge. Show them exactly what you are doing and what your intentions are. This makes you even more powerful.

CHAPTER 5

Define Your Own Meaning of "Great"

Even as an adult, it can be difficult to define the meaning of the word "great." What does this mean to you right now? It might mean being a mother who is always there for her children and present for every school function. It could also mean being the employee who always stays late at the office and is willing to go the extra mile. Greatness can be defined in so many ways which is why you need to figure out what it means to you. It is clear that you want to be great, but it must be clear what you think of when you hear that word.

Avoiding Bad Influences

A bad influence is merely somebody who takes up your time in a negative manner. When you were younger, this could have been the playground bully or a friend who always encouraged you to disobey your parents. Now that you are a parent and a responsible adult, you have probably forgotten about these bad influences that used to be so convincing back then. What you do not realize is that they are still present—they just take on different forms than they used to. What you must learn is how to guard your energy and to only use it on people, places, and situations that are going to benefit you and make you an even better version of yourself.

There are five main things that you can do in life to avoid bad influences and keep your energy pure. This is going to ensure that you are focused on your tasks and what matters most to you. Negativity can take away a lot of your concentration but also valuable time with the ones you love. As long as you are aware of your habits, you should be able to figure out ways to rid your life of any of the negativity that remains.

Guard Your Time

It is easy for negative people to take over your time. They have a tendency to do so because they do not value their own. This means that they will have no problem taking advantage of yours, even when you have priorities to attend to. Watch out for these time-consuming vultures because they can slip into your life just as easily as you decide that you will give them a little extra time here and there—it all adds up! Before you know it, you will not even have time to spend on yourself. Having alone time to decompress is just as important as having time to work on your goals.

When you can feel that somebody is doing this to you, even if it is somebody you love and respect, you need to create some boundaries. Do not let them take up all of your time and energy. Do not complain about them to others or start a confrontation. You can purposely and intentionally make yourself busy so that you do not appear to have the free time for them to steal. For example, set aside this free time to work on your goals or to play with your children. When you make yourself less available, these energy vampires will stay far away from you because they will realize that you have other things happening in your life.

Choose Your Attitude

One of the easiest ways to kill your good mood is by spending time with negative people. Those you spend the most time around become the people you model your behavior after. Without even realizing it, you are going to pick up on these nuances and negative behaviors yourself. This is going to ultimately bring you down and make you feel like you cannot accomplish your tasks. Take a good look at who you have been spending your time around lately.

You cannot always choose your company, but make it a point to take control when you can. This is going to give you the motivation necessary to create a positive attitude that surrounds you with determination. No matter what you are doing, this positive attitude will carry you through to the next task effortlessly. In turn, you are also going to be positively influencing those that are around you.

Even an attitude that is not necessarily negative can come across as a negative influence. If you have ever met someone with a dismissive attitude, this might be influencing you more than you realize. By the other person dismissing opportunities, you might feel tempted to do the same and will end up missing out on great situations that can lead you even closer to your goals. The thing about working hard is that you never want to automatically dismiss something—feel it out; see how it might benefit you first.

Create a mantra that you will choose to follow when you can tell that someone is being negative, dismissive, or any other type of way that is not going to make you a successful person. Tell yourself that you can choose your own attitude, and you can choose who you are influenced by. If someone does not make you feel good, this is an indication that you probably need to spend less time around them. No matter what anyone else around you is doing, stay focused on your goals. Understand that you have to take your own path to reach your desired end results.

Refocus Your Thoughts

You might believe that you are in control of the way that you think, but negative people can infiltrate your subconscious. This is going to distract you without you even realizing it. Instead of thinking about what someone else is doing, thinking, or saying, you need to set this intention on your own actions. If you notice that another person is showing off or trying to outdo you, then let them do their thing. This is the easiest way to handle people who only want to be negative and bring you down. When you do not feed into their game, they will not get any satisfaction from it.

Think about what you can try to do to improve your performance. This does not have to involve anyone else's actions because you need to do what is best for you. Try to focus on your end result and really make it a point to not let anything else stand in your way. When you refocus your thoughts, your entire mindset is going to change. You will notice that everything is going to feel easier and more fulfilling as you work on it. A hardworking mother is always a big thinker, but you need to go above and beyond this goal—you must refocus on something that is going to lead you to the end result that you crave.

If you notice your thoughts changing, pay attention to this. You should make sure you are not changing them because you are being influenced by others around you. It is normal for your thoughts to fluctuate because of your mood, but they should not be as altered by other people if you can help it. Work on being an independent thinker, only allowing yourself to think about the tasks and actions that are going to benefit you and your future. Remember that mental energy is just as valuable as physical energy. You need to guard it in the same exact way. If you can feel that yours is being depleted, take inventory of what you are spending it on. Delegate tasks, and do what you can to replenish it.

Choose to Be Productive

One thing that you are probably forgetting is that you have a choice when it comes to productivity. You get to seek out this behavior for yourself and implement it. This does not require you to be told that you must complete a task or take action—self-discipline is extremely necessary when it comes to productivity. When you are at home, nobody is going to be telling you to get all of the chores done and make sure that the kids have clean clothes to wear to school—these are tasks that you must be responsible for keeping track of. You need to prove to yourself that you can create a schedule and stick to it.

It can be very tempting to blame negative people for your behavior when you are slacking off. Blaming others is a natural response when you are not making progress because you do not want to admit that it is your doing. You do not want to admit that your actions have caused you to fall behind or to not meet your goals. This is a habit that you can change by taking accountability for all of your actions, both good and bad. Make a commitment to controlling your emotions and realizing that things do not always have to be as negative as others might make them out to be. With your decision to react or to keep moving forward, you are either going to set yourself up for failure or success.

When you realize how much control you have over your reactions, it is both empowering and freeing. You get to decide if something or someone is worth your time and energy. Being productive is a choice, just like being a hard worker and a great mother. Think of this task as you would the other two. It is a guarantee that you will be willing to work a lot harder when you view things this way. Always remember to stay true to your values—this will help you ensure that you are on the right path. If it makes you feel good inside, then you should have a positive outward response.

Seek Out Positive People

You should always be on the lookout for positive influences to accept into your life. The people that you have in your life now might be very positive, but there is always room for more positivity. Be open to meeting and interacting with new people. You never know who you are going to encounter that might end up changing your mindset for the better. The more positivity you have in your life, the more motivated and productive you will feel. By putting out the energy that you want to attract only positive people and positive things, you should see this reflected in the interactions that you have daily.

When you are not surrounded by other people, you can make a commitment to yourself. Commit to being the best version of yourself possible and the most positive person you can be. This is going to allow you to exude even more of the wonderful energy that you wish to attract. Everything comes full circle when it comes to positivity. Remember that the energy never stops, even when you stop thinking about it. The energy is always going to surround you and reflect in the behavior that you exhibit. Ignorance is not bliss like most people seem to think.

Consciousness is the key to being the best version of yourself that you can possibly be. You must be purposeful and intentional. Give yourself time to really get to know the person that you have become and what your goals are. You are going to change over time, so doing this often is going to be very helpful. Teach yourself that you are going to keep changing, and this is okay. You will get the chance to grow and evolve, adjusting your behaviors and maybe even your core values. It is much better to change than to remain stagnant for years on end. Not all change has to be bad or scary—it can actually be one of the greatest ways to seek out new and positive people in your life.

Achieving Greatness

Now that you have defined greatness, how are you going to get there? You need to plan this out; think about how you are going to work through all of the procrastination and the unwillingness to go the extra mile. With these tips, you are going to see that you can achieve even more greatness than you ever thought possible. Try them out for yourself; see the difference that they make in your life and in your mindset.

1. Create a Bright Vision

Always make sure that your vision is clear. Make it exciting and vibrant. If you create a vision for your life that is not exciting to you, then you are not going to feel motivated to complete it. A vision does not always have to be rigid and structured. It can be a lot of fun if you put enough thought into it. Vision boards do help, and making them whenever you feel like you have new goals is going to be ideal for you. Go with the flow, and recognize that you have the ability to change your mind and go after new things.

Talk about your vision whenever you can! When you can tell other people about what it is that you want and what you are doing to get there, this is going to make the vision seem even more exciting. Explain it in detail to those who support you and who are willing to listen. By going through all of the steps, this also serves as a reminder that it is possible to think of new steps that you can take. As you explain them to other people, this could lead you to some pretty great epiphanies that will make your journey a lot easier and more successful. Keep an open mind when it comes to your vision.

Sometimes, things are not going to work according to plan, but you will still be able to reach the same end result.

2. Turn Adversity Into Advantage

The adversity that you have been through in life does not define you, but it does impact the way you think about your goals and success. When something brings you down, it is natural to feel upset about it. You might be fearful that the same thing will happen to you again, but you cannot let this mentality hold you back. Choose to see your adversity as a turning point that you can use to your advantage—you can try to do this by thinking that you already know what to do if the same thing goes wrong again. You are more prepared than you were before.

It is normal to want to sulk about the bad things that have happened to you in life, but you do not need to stay in this mindset forever. Let yourself have a moment to process the negativity, then tell yourself that you are going to bypass it. Prove to yourself that you can move on from it with ease, and you are going to be more successful than ever. This mentality works, and the more you do it, the better you will truly get at it. Everybody is going to go through some adversity in life. Without it, we would not be able to learn any great life lessons. Be thankful for all that it has taught you and how well it has prepared you. Your weaknesses are about to become strengths!

3. Cultivate a Champion's Mindset

Even if you are not a competitive person, you need to become more motivated than you currently are. Challenge yourself! Give yourself a chance to prove that you can really become a champion if you want to. Not everybody has an easy time getting into this mindset, but it does help when you are trying to achieve greatness. It is possible to teach yourself how to get into a better mindset by observing how other champions operate. Take a look at how those you admire live their lives. You can end up learning a lot by seeing how they stay motivated and what keeps them moving forward.

A little healthy competition is good for you. If there is someone you work with that holds the same title, there is nothing wrong with wanting to stand out to your boss or wanting to put in a little extra effort because you want to cultivate your champion's mindset. As long as you are playing fair, then encourage yourself to make more opportunities like these. Be competitive in a way that drives motivation from the other person, as well. Think about the last time that you have achieved greatness—this depends on how you view it and how you view your accomplishments. Remember how great this felt and how you want to return to this feeling again and again.

4. Use Your Hustle

You have probably heard the term before, but believe in yourself and your ability to use it! You have hustle by being a mom and a successful businesswoman. You can do both of these tasks simultaneously, and this proves that you have the determination and courage that make up for the "hustle" that so many admire and want in their own lives. If you are going to do great things, there is no need to be shy about it. Make sure that you celebrate your successes and tell people when there is cause for celebration. You deserve to do this, and you are going to realize that your hustle is going to be a major driving force in your life.

One way to bring out your hustle is by telling your story to someone who is willing to listen. You can even tell your children. Teach them what you have been through and all of the adversity that you have faced along the way. Show them where you are now and why this is an accomplishment and a real-life example of success. You are going to remember things that you probably forgot you went through, and this will drive you to hustle even harder. Think about how strong you are and how much you have already gone through—this means that there is no stopping now. You can keep going—hustling and working harder than ever before.

5. Master Your Body

You might be wondering what your body has to do with your accomplishments and achieving greatness. It has a lot to do with this because of the way that you are able to function or not function. When you pay attention to how your body feels overall, you are going to save yourself from the burnout that so many hardworking moms reach as they try to do too many things at one time. Master all of the cues that your body sends you, and pay attention when you feel that you are approaching a breaking point. Without a healthy and working body, you are not going to be able to achieve anything. There is a difference between pushing yourself in a competitive way and pushing yourself to the point of no return.

One of the best ways to master your body is by taking time for yourself. Listen to your cues, and see what makes you feel good. This is why self-care is so essential to this entire process. You will be able to determine what your body needs when you are happy, sad, stressed, and anything in between. As long as you are always willing to pay attention to this, then you will be able to give yourself everything that you require to remain the most functional and best version of yourself. Remember that food is fuel—keep your tank full! Drink plenty of water because hydration is essential to keeping all of your bodily systems working.

6. **Practice Great Habits**

Forming habits is easy, but keeping them is a little harder. You need to commit to keeping them in your life and maintaining them. Once you figure out the habits that are considered great and productive, you must cling to them tightly. Imagine how you can use them on a daily basis so that they become a part of your regular routine. It is going to feel like more work at first, but you will get used to this process. Soon enough, it is going to feel natural. You will be glad that you made the commitment to taking on more positive habits in your life.

Use your bad habits to motivate you! Instead of feeling bad about the negative habits that you currently have, you can use them as the driving force behind creating even better ones. Think about all of the aspects of these habits that you do not like. Consider the negativity they bring into your life. This is why you need a change, and this is why you are going to feel motivated to create better ones that will stick. You can learn a lot from yourself by paying attention to your bad habits. With any habit, it is not going to become permanent unless you make the decision to let it. You have this power, and this is always something that you should remember.

7. Build a Winning Team

Choosing to achieve greatness on your own is always an option, but do not forget that you can create a winning team. This team can consist of your peers and even your family. A team is simply a group of people who want the same end result as you. When you have a team that is on your side, this is going to motivate you even more. You will feel like you cannot let the other people on your team down, and this will allow your creativity to be unleashed. Show your team how hard you are willing to work and what you are capable of, even if they do not demand this from you.

A winning team should consist of people who want the same things that you want. They should all be positive individuals who value success and greatness, just like you. Make sure that you are a part of the right team because you know how easily the wrong people can hold you back. Step up, and be a leader of this winning team. Encourage your family to do more chores together and your peers to work harder on projects together. This will help you with your personal and professional goals by keeping you more organized. Other people on your team will complement your weaknesses. What you lack, other people will probably have. They can help you and uplift you.

8. Live a Life of Service

Achieving greatness is possible through acts of service. If you feel that you cannot help yourself, make it a point to do something kind for someone else. This is still greatness, and it will make you feel like you are doing something productive with your time. There are a few ways that you can easily go about this, and one of them is by doing a five-minute favor for someone. Think about a favor that you can do that will only take five minutes of time. This can be helping someone unload their groceries or even paying for the person behind you in line at the coffee shop. All of these little good deeds add up in big ways.

Make acting out of service and kindness your lifestyle, not just something that you do because you know it is good to do. Once you start, you will enjoy it tremendously. There are always kindness options for every situation you find yourself in. Even just addressing someone who is going through a difficult time or struggling can make all the difference in that person's life. You never know how much your words and actions can touch another person. Keep an open mind, and try to be there for anyone you can when you have the emotional capacity to do so. This kindness will find its way back to you in your life.

These tips are meant to guide you and to help you. Use them as you see fit, and make sure that you vary them. Nobody likes to follow the same boring, mundane routine. You will probably do a lot better with your accomplishments when you can switch up the tasks that you are doing and these strategies that you will implement to help you get there.

CHAPTER 6

Boundaries: How to Set Them

As a mother, you might feel obligated to say yes to everything and anything that you are asked to do. There are many tasks that you just have to endure when you are a mother, but there are also opportunities to set personal boundaries for yourself. This might seem against the grain at first, but you need to remember that even you have your limits. Setting boundaries is healthy for both you and your family. When they realize that you cannot do everything at any time, you are going to feel more respected and valued as a mother. Setting boundaries does not have to feel like a punishment or something negative. It can become a way for you to delegate tasks when you just cannot take on any more responsibilities.

Household Boundaries

Remember that you do *not* always have to say yes. In society, it is common to believe that you need to say yes or you will be viewed as a bad mother, but this is untrue. You get to define how you view yourself, so you get to define what makes a good mother. If you are unable to get to a task or to complete something, it is best to just be honest. Communicate with your family, and get help from your partner—this is what they should be here for. By delegating tasks to your partner, this will get them more involved in the responsibilities while also making sure that every task still gets done.

You can also delegate tasks to your children. Depending on how old they are, it is a good life lesson to teach them how to take on responsibilities. This takes a load off of your back while simultaneously teaching them necessary life skills. In some ways, this is also how you are going to set boundaries for yourself. Teach your children how hard work can get them far in life and why it is important to keep trying. When you stay motivated, they will be more willing to stay motivated and to keep up their end of the bargain. Doing chores and having roles really helps any family dynamic.

Setting boundaries is not setting an ultimatum. This is an extreme way to view boundaries that society has been teaching you since you became a mother. Boundaries are healthy—they keep you sane. Even your children will need them at times, but you need to make a great example of this by setting them for yourself first. Your partner might even forget that boundaries are healthy, so you can make this a teachable moment for them, as well. Start off small. Ask for 10 minutes of alone time each day. This is a realistic boundary that almost every mother should be able to set.

With this boundary, you can do anything you like. It is your time, so use it as you wish. You can use it to relax or to plan out the next activities that you must do—anything that you want! During your alone time, it should be noted that everyone in your family is going to respect your privacy. You should be able to go to a quiet space and just have this time to yourself without interruptions. When you view boundaries this way, you will see that they do not have to be so extreme.

Even something so small can make a huge difference, and you will feel a lot less stressed out about your daily tasks when you have even 10 more minutes to yourself each day.

This task might seem easier said than done, but you will get there. You can use the following tips to help enforce this practice and to normalize setting boundaries while you are at home:

- If you have a home office, place a sign on your door that says "busy" or "do not disturb." This is a friendly way to show your family that you are in the middle of something. When this sign is on your door, teach your family that this means you require privacy. Unless it is an emergency, they should not have to come get you or knock on your door. This uninterrupted time is going to be so valuable to you as a mother.
- Communicate clearly. Explain to your children why you need privacy and space sometimes. When you can make it apparent that it has nothing to do with them or that it just helps you concentrate, they will not take it as personally. Use simple language, and make sure that they understand this is not some form of punishment because of their actions.
- Make sure that your children understand that certain areas of the home might be off-limits at times. This can mean your bedroom or your office—just any space that you require privacy in. Teach them these boundaries at a young age, and the information will be retained. If they grow up knowing this, then it will

not come as such a shock when you tell them that they cannot come in right at that moment.
- Allow your children to feel that there are consequences when a boundary is broken. For example, if you ask for privacy and the kids keep opening your office door, you can discipline them as you see fit. Make sure that they understand this is not a game or something to be taken lightly. A boundary should always be respected, just as you will always respect their boundaries. Teach children that "no" means "no" the first time.

How to Stop Feeling Guilty

Even if you set healthy boundaries in your household, you are probably going to feel guilty at times. You want to be open and honest with your children, giving them everything. Understand that your time and energy is precious, and you deserve some of it for yourself. Part of the reason you likely feel so guilty is that the media portrays mothers and motherhood as this entity that is always 100% on. You need to always be there for your children, ignoring all of your needs to please them—this just is not realistic. You need balance if you want to have a happy family dynamic. If you only put them first, you get burned out. If you only put yourself first, they feel neglected. This is why balance is so essential and why balance will allow you to let go of any guilt you are holding on to.

Think about simpler times before social media and other digital societal influences. Do you think that these mothers also worried about their children and if they were good enough mothers? Of course they did. This is a universal feeling that has been around for many centuries. What you are feeling is normal, and what you worry about just enforces the point that you are a great mom. You cannot always do everything, but you can always do your best. This is more than good enough, and you should give yourself credit for it.

If you are struggling with guilt during the process of setting boundaries, try to turn a blind eye to social media and what other mothers around you are doing. You ultimately need to do what is best for you and your family. Each household is going to vary, and it is unfair to compare your own to anyone else's household. You need to do what is fair for you, and you will discover this by the process of trial and error. See what works, and take note of what does not. You will soon find your perfect balance and understand exactly how you need to create your boundaries.

What Your Children Will Learn

By teaching your children boundaries at a young age, it will allow them to appreciate what they have and all of the privileges they receive. If you were to tell them yes to anything and everything they wanted, they would grow up feeling entitled and probably act bratty. Getting told "no" is a humbling experience that they must be prepared to face. This is going to happen to them during childhood, all the way into adulthood. They must learn how to take this with a humble stride and how to accept it by moving forward in a respectful manner. When they understand why a boundary is in place and how it will help them, they will be less likely to challenge it.

Through you setting boundaries, your children will also learn how to eventually set their own. When they are not okay with something, they will feel more inspired to speak up about it and to explain how it makes them feel. This is crucial, especially when you are not always there to protect them from all of the bad things in the world. They need to be able to hold their own and to set boundaries when they feel like they are in danger or possibly being intruded upon. Having a real-life example from their mother is the best way to learn.

Mental health is also a very important topic to touch on when you are raising a child. You need to show them that they can protect their mental health by setting clear boundaries. Even if they need to set them in regard to something you are doing, then this is going to help them see that they can protect their mental health. By respecting them, then you are also showing them that you care about them. They are also going to learn how to respect other people in the process.

Workplace Boundaries

Discussing household boundaries is important, but learning how to set workplace boundaries is equally important. You need to realize that these boundaries can exist, even if you are not a supervisor or manager. As an employee, you must always feel valued and cared for. If you feel that you are not being treated fairly, speak up about it! So many women go along with certain treatment because they believe that they have to endure it. If they do not go with it, then they worry that they are going to lose their status or respectability.

Use these methods to help you maintain your workplace boundaries. They can all help you in different ways, and they will make sure that you are being treated fairly when you are in a professional setting.

1. Seek Help When Necessary

Whenever you need help creating boundaries, ask for advice! Talk to your boss on a person-to-person level. They might be able to give you some valuable insight that will make you feel more confident in your decision making. Make sure you know exactly what you are being held accountable for in your current position, and run this list by your boss to ensure you are on the same page. This will show you a lot about what you might need to change or what you might need to do slightly differently.

After looking at this list of responsibilities, see which ones are your priorities. Place stars next to the ones that are the most important. This is what will teach you how to focus. It might be an eye-opening experience to see which goals you have right now.

This is also going to make a healthy impact on your interactions with your peers, as well. You can learn how to ask them for help. See what they are doing at work, and see if any of these behaviors can positively impact your workplace boundaries.

2. Conduct an Audit

Along with approaching your boss or supervisor for advice, you should also conduct an audit of the people you work with. When you feel that your boundaries are feeling crossed, you need to take note of this. See if this is a pattern that you notice while you are working. If you do notice that it is a pattern that particular people are displaying, you definitely need to have a conversation with them about your boundaries and why this behavior is unacceptable to you.

If you notice yourself feeling angry, resentful, or even guilty, then you should definitely pay close attention to this. Your workplace should not feel like a stressful environment. You can have conversations that are not confrontational with your peers to establish your boundaries. By using "I" statements, you will be able to approach them without making them feel angry.

By conducting an audit, this does not necessarily mean that you have to cut communication with certain peers at the office. What this means is that you just need to preserve your energy by setting boundaries. In your free time, you do not need to associate with them or have banter, inside or outside of work, with them if that is not what you are comfortable with.

You do not have any obligations to your peers outside of your responsibilities, and it can take a lot of stress off your plate when you set these professional boundaries. You are not necessarily there to make friends. You are there to do your job to the best of your ability. The friendships and connections that are formed are just extras.

3. **Set Your Limits**

Just as you did at home, you will set your limits at work. When you get an idea of the areas you would like to particularly focus on when setting your boundaries, you can create limits that will support these areas. For example, if you find yourself getting distracted by banter often, tell all of your peers that you need quiet time between certain hours of the day. This will ensure that you are able to get all of your work done without getting distracted.

Make it clear if you want to socialize during other times, but also establish these times and when it will feel okay for you to take a moment for socialization. Some people can work while they talk and others cannot. You do not have to go with the flow just because everyone else is doing it. Work the way that you need to work in order to be successful.

Another boundary that you should set is the boundary between your time spent working and time spent off. When you are not at work, you should not be thinking at work. Your management should be respectful of this desire to have a personal life and to have family time. If you feel that you are constantly worrying about work and trying to work when you are not even on the clock, a better boundary needs to be set to prevent this.

4. **Communicate Clearly**

After you set your boundaries, you must communicate on a regular basis! If someone is not respecting them, then you need to tell them. Sometimes, it takes several reminders before someone gets the hint. This can be the unfortunate but necessary part of setting boundaries. You need to speak up about them, or else nobody is going to observe them. Do not feel guilty for reminding someone of your own personal boundaries—this is your right in the workplace.

Do not skirt around the subject, either. Being direct is always the better option because you will not run into any misunderstandings. If you only hint at there being a crossed boundary, then the other person might not get it right away. You will have to do double the work by reminding them another time. If you are direct about how this crossing of the boundary makes you feel, it will sink in a lot faster.

Your peers must respect you as much as you respect yourself, and this includes your management team. Just because you rank lower than other people at your job does not mean that your feelings should go ignored. You are only human, and this is something that should be taken into account when interacting with anyone at any time. Make sure that you are being treated fairly, and stand up for yourself when you are not.

5. Delegate More Tasks

You can be a leader even when that exact role has not been assigned to you. Just as you delegate tasks at home, you will also have to delegate tasks at work. Instead of letting yourself feel stressed out all the time because of what you must do, see if you can gather help from your peers to get everything finished. If someone is pulling less weight than others on the team, you should not feel guilty for asking them to take on certain tasks that you know you do not have time to do.

Asking for help should not feel shameful. It is a smart and efficient way to work, especially when you already know how much you are able to handle. Delegating tasks ensures that all of the work gets done when it is supposed to, and this is something that your management team will probably recognize in a great way. They will see that you are a fast thinker and a pragmatic worker.

Even if you are uncomfortable in a leadership role right now, this is a skill that can be learned. You can teach yourself how to be more confident in the workplace by reminding yourself of your worth. What are the skills that you excel at? These skills make you the wonderful employee that you are, and they show you how valuable you are. Build up on this self-confidence by constantly reminding yourself of how great you are.

6. Take Time to Respond

A trick that you can use that will help you with setting boundaries is taking a moment to respond. If you choose to respond instantly every time, you are more likely to say "yes." Take enough time to think clearly about what is being asked of you. See if it makes sense to even say yes to this in the first place. When you pause like this, you will save yourself a lot of hassle and energy because you will be able to give an answer that aligns with your work ethic and boundaries.

Not every question requires a time-sensitive answer. You take back some of the power when you can tell the other person that you need a minute to consider it. Take as much time as you need when there is no deadline in place. This is going to help you set boundaries that you might not even realize you need. It is a technique that you are going to begin using in your personal life, as well.

You can tell someone that you need a moment to check your schedule and that you will get back to them. This puts you in the position to get back to them on your own time with your own values in mind. Consider your priorities and what you have going on in your professional life. If you encounter any conflicts, then you might need to see if there are certain boundaries you need to implement before making your final decision.

7. Practice Saying "No"

It can be very hard to deny someone something, especially when someone asks you a direct question that does not allow you the time to think about your answer. You might feel pressured to say yes right away because you have been conditioned to believe that saying no is impolite. You have every right to say no, and it is a complete answer. This does not have to be something confrontational or even personal. If it does not work with your schedule, then you can say no— it's that simple.

Practice saying it at any chance you get. If you truly do not want to do something, then say no. Do not feel guilty for saying no because you have the right to make this choice. You truly know how much time and energy you are working with, as well as the tasks on your to-do list. You should make sure that you are putting your professional priorities first— this is a very admirable trait that will make you stand out from the crowd.

It can even be helpful when you practice saying "no" in front of a mirror to yourself. Saying the word aloud can feel foreign if you are not used to saying it at all. By just practicing reciting it, you will feel a lot more capable of saying it in the correct context in the future. Give it a try the next time that you have a moment to yourself.

8. Develop a System

Productivity expert, David Allen, has created a system that you can follow to ensure that you are keeping up with all of your limits and boundaries while at work. As you sort through your to-do list, think about the following steps ("The 4 Ds of Time Management," n.d.):

- Do it
- Defer it
- Delegate it
- Drop it

These are your four options when presented with a task. You will either get it done as you should, pass it along to someone else, or stop spending your time and energy on it because it does not matter to your professional life.

While you do not have to use this system exactly as it is presented, it will make for a great foundation on which you can base your own system off of. Make sure that the system makes sense for the way you work and the way you prioritize your tasks. You will feel a lot more organized when you know that there are only a few options to select for any given task or situation that comes up while you are working.

Being systematic helps you to stay motivated. This is going to create a very focused and streamlined approach to your work, no matter what industry you are in. Your superiors are surely going to notice this extra effort you are putting in. The best part is that it will not feel like extra work because it is actually going to make your life easier and save you time.

9. Create Structure

If you feel like you are being driven crazy by your long days and time-consuming meetings, take a moment to breathe. You need to create a structure for yourself so you do not reach a point of burnout. Create an agenda that you can stick to. An agenda is basically just a schedule with an intention. It has all of your tasks on it, plus the timelines that you want to adhere to. It also involves your personal values and priorities.

When you have an agenda, you also have more control of what you are doing during your workday. Your agenda will become your guideline, and you can refer to it when you are feeling overwhelmed or confused about what to do next. There is a lot of power behind this kind of leadership, and it is great because it does not involve telling others what they need to do. This type of leadership is self-leadership, and it is important to practice.

Have a weekly check-in with yourself to make sure that your agenda is still giving you the structure that you desire. You need to make sure that it is still working because your feelings can change. Your tasks are also bound to change. This is something that you need to take into consideration, and you need to make sure that it is still working for you. Even if your boss always pops in to check on you, you'll still need to have your own time to make sure that you are working in the most efficient way possible.

10. Prepare for Some Pushback

Once you start applying your healthy workplace boundaries, you can expect some pushback. Whether this comes from yourself internally or others who just do not understand why you are not being as open as usual, you can expect for this to happen. When you do, it will make you more likely to be able to handle the pushback rather than question your boundaries and let go of them as easily.

Keep an eye on those who react negatively to your boundaries. These are the people who do not truly support you or respect you. Anybody who cares will want you to be the best version of yourself possible, and this does involve making some small sacrifices if necessary. Even if you believe that these people mean well, you should still pay attention to those who give you any negative type of pushback.

The most productive and happiest employees are the ones who set boundaries for themselves. They are the ones who are able to separate their emotions from the work that is ahead of them. You need to remind yourself that you are one of these successful women. You have all of the strength necessary to make this a reality for yourself, and you will start to understand this more by the way that you set boundaries for yourself at work.

CHAPTER 7

Clarifying Your Emotions

Emotional clarity is such a necessity, and you are going to learn how to obtain this for yourself no matter what you are doing and where you are. You have been learning how to manage both of your very important roles in your life, but you need to always keep in mind that your emotions should be clarified and processed as soon as possible. Your emotional clarity is simply a way of saying that you understand the thoughts in your head. You understand how they can lead to certain behaviors and actions on your behalf. It is a very personal process to go through, but you will learn how to do this effortlessly.

As a mother and a worker, you are going to experience so many emotions in your life. A lot of them get cast aside because you have other things to do, but you should make it a point to return to these emotions when you have the time. You need to work on processing them and seeing where they are truly coming from. Getting to the root of the issue is going to be the best option because you will be able to solve the problem from the source. Teach yourself that you are only human; it is okay to experience a wide variety of emotions, even when you are taking care of the kids or completing your tasks at work.

One thing you are not is a robot, so you should not treat yourself like one. If you feel emotions at a time when you cannot just stop and clarify, try to remember this feeling for later. Jot down a quick note about it if you can. Any small step that you take toward clarifying your emotions and reminding yourself of them is going to make you an even better mother because you will be more emotionally available to your children and partner. This is also going to affect the way that you work because you will be better able to focus on your tasks with a clearer mind.

Steps to Take

There are a plethora of steps for you to take to better manage your emotions. When they are simply laid out, they will not seem as overwhelming to you. See if you can apply these steps to your life regardless of what you are doing and what role you are in. They apply to both your personal life and your professional life.

- **Label Your Emotions With Plain Language**

There is no use in making complex situations even more complex than they need to be. Use plain language when you are handling your emotions. If you are feeling sad, accept that sadness is the emotion. You are going to clarify it soon, but you can simply place a plain label on it to start. The same can even be done with positive emotions. Teach yourself that you do not need to scrutinize your emotions or make things complicated—this is only going to overwhelm you and cause you to overthink when you already do not have this capacity.

To practice labeling your emotions, take this quick screening. Set a timer for 60 seconds, and try to name as many emotions as you can in this time. You can use this chart to gauge how well you are doing with recognizing emotions and how well you are able to identify them in yourself.

20+: Well above average

14+: Above average

10: Average

<7: Below average

This scale is not meant to make you feel bad about yourself or to make you feel inadequate, but it will give you a rough idea of how well you are able to identify emotions and how well you are understanding yourself.

If your number is lower than you imagined, you do not have to view this negatively. Think of this as an opportunity to make progress. You can teach yourself how to label your emotions. Write down all of the emotions you can think of by doing the exercise again. Refer to this piece of paper when you are having trouble placing your own—it helps to organize them. At the very least, you can organize them by negative and positive emotions. This will give you some structure.

- **Train Yourself to See Emotional Complexity**

As you start to learn more about the different emotions that you are capable of feeling, you are going to train yourself to view emotional complexity as something that is normal. While you might be able to label them simply, they can blend together and turn into anomalies that you are unaware of at first. Try not to let this get you down. Think about how every emotion can stem from a basic emotion that you have already learned. What happens next is complexity, but it is something that you can work through.

When you feel negative or upset, you automatically assume that you are feeling one single emotion. You place all of your weight on this emotion, but this is often not what is going on. Emotions are complex, and they can evolve instantly. Depending on what triggered you in the first place, you might be experiencing a bunch of emotions without even realizing it. Try to deconstruct what you are feeling by starting with the base emotion. If you are annoyed at work, you can place your focus on this annoyance. It is negative and something you would rather not feel. What can you do to go even deeper?

Try to break your annoyance down into three more emotions. Ask yourself what triggered you or what is causing you to feel annoyed. Once you do this, you are going to see that there is a lot more going on than you realize. You might be surprised by what rises to the surface, but welcome them with open arms. You are on your way to understanding their complexity and to understanding the way that you truly feel.

- **Feel Your Emotions Physically**

Most emotions draw out physical feelings if you are willing to take them. Many people believe they need to suppress them because it seems wrong to feel emotional and physically affected. Train yourself to explore these physical feelings. They might be able to teach you a lot more about what you are truly going through. Show yourself that you are not afraid to feel things physically, and you are able to work through these symptoms because you have learned how to take care of your body. This all cycles back to self-care.

Of course, you need to pay close attention to any negative physical symptoms that you feel. If you are feeling a little light-headed, maybe you need to drink some water or have a snack. If you have a lot of tension in your body, maybe you need to work on some breathing exercises until you can get home and receive a massage from your partner. There are always ways that you can work on making yourself feel better physically, even when you cannot devote all of your time toward self-care at that moment.

On the other hand, make sure that you can also recognize that there will be times when your physical symptoms have nothing to do with your emotions. If you are feeling generally positive emotions and you have a headache, this might be a regular and unrelated headache. By always keeping an open mind, you will teach yourself when you need to dissect these physical symptoms and when you just need to let them be. This becomes part of your system and a part of the steps that you choose to take. You will get better at this the more that you practice doing this, just like anything in life.

- **Time Your Emotions**

If you come to work feeling like you are already stressed out, this is something that you might be able to time. It sounds crazy, but it is possible to time your emotions sometimes. If you already know that you are having a hard or bad day, you need to realize that you might have to put these emotions aside while you are at work or taking care of your children until you have some privacy to deal with them.

This is not to say that you are going to suppress anything, but you will put them on hold until you can have the proper time to work on them.

Realizing that you can do this will empower you greatly. You will see that you do not have to succumb to the things that you are feeling when you are dealing with your busy life. Of course, it will not always be possible to control your emotions in this way, but it is always worth a try when you know that something is already wrong. See if you can set your focus on something positive that will get you through your day until you can return to your emotions.

Another way that you can time your emotions is by looking at them as something that is temporary. Set an actual timer on your phone, and sit in the current emotion you are feeling for three minutes. This is your time to dwell, stew, and feel negatively about the situation. Once this timer is up, set a focus on moving forward. See if you can switch what you are feeling by turning it into something more productive. There is nothing wrong with sitting in your negativity temporarily, but you should make sure that you can move past the feeling.

- **Learn About Your Emotional Weakness**

There is usually one trigger that will always make you upset in any situation. This could be something that pertains to a situation or event that you have gone through in the past, and it causes you to feel weak. Giving an example of this can be difficult because it is such a personal weakness. This all depends on your life, what you have seen, and how you have dealt with it. You need to identify this particular weakness because it is likely going to pop up when you least expect it.

After you know what triggers you, this gives you the power to avoid it when you are unable to deal with the emotions. By putting them on hold and avoiding this trigger, you are actually doing yourself a favor by allowing yourself to focus on better things. You will be able to learn how to compartmentalize these things temporarily and how to return to them later.

This weakness is usually something that causes you to make bad decisions or to take impulsive actions. No matter what you are doing, this weakness can appear to attempt to derail you, but you do not have to let this happen. By identifying it and learning that you can always come back to it, it will no longer rule over you as it once did.

Avoidance is not what you should be aiming for with your weakness. You need to realize that it is okay to put something on pause and to return to it. You are a busy and hardworking mom, so it is not uncommon that you are just going to be busy sometimes. When you get alone time, you can revisit the weakness and see what must be done about it.

- **Validate Your Emotions**

This seems like a very simple step, but it can be a lot harder than you realize. Validating your emotions is hard because you expect this from other people. You want to make others proud, and you want to hear this validation from your family or superiors at work. You will not always hear this validation when you need it, so you need to become comfortable with the idea that you can validate them on your own. You can give yourself the power that you need.

Any emotion that you are feeling is valid, no matter if it makes sense to you or not at the moment. You will learn how to dissect it and how to process it. In the meantime, validate yourself—teach yourself that it is okay to feel anything that you are feeling. You are only a human being, and your emotions are not always going to make sense at first. This is okay because you are going to make an effort to understand them.

When you get validation from others, this is great! Remember these compliments, and try to use them on yourself when you do not have someone next to you cheering you on. You can learn a lot about yourself based on the way that others view you. It might surprise you just how strong you are and how amazing you are perceived by those around you.

Human beings get into the habit of treating their emotions like problems, but this is not true. Even your worst emotions are not problems. They matter because you are feeling them. If they go unaddressed, they are not going anywhere. You will only internalize them, making yourself feel worse. Learn how to let go of them and how to truly process them in a healthy way.

All of these steps are very valuable to remember. You need to keep in mind that they are going to help you at different times depending on what you are going through, so try them all at some point. See which ones feel right to you.

The Key Points

As you work on your journey of emotional clarity, there are several key points that you should focus on. Many thoughts are going to come to mind, but you need to sort through them in a way that is productive to you and your life. You live a busy life, and you do not always have the time to go through every single thought for hours at a time—this is also unhealthy. Teach yourself that you can sift through the thoughts until you are able to find the most relevant and important ones. Think about what makes something important to you.

1. Does it affect your family?

2. Does it affect your job?

3. Does it affect your feelings?

With these three basic questions, you should likely be able to determine if a thought is worth the exploration. When you can answer yes to one of the above questions, you should explore the feeling and try to further clarify the emotion. When you do this, you are not doing it to appease anyone else: You are doing it because you deserve this clarity for yourself.

- Having good emotional vocabulary is going to help you tremendously. When you have plenty of labels to place on your emotions, this is going to help you identify what you are experiencing and what you might go through as a result of them. Having this vocabulary is going to make it a lot easier to think clearly about your emotions.

- It is very rare that you are going to experience one emotion at a time. At any given point, you are probably experiencing multiple emotions. This presents you with more of a challenge when it comes to sorting through this, but keeping this in mind will teach you that it is possible to sift through the most important ones.
- Since so many negative emotions can result in physical consequences, you need to be aware of which physical symptoms are being caused by your negative emotions and which ones have nothing to do with them. By truly knowing your body and understanding how you operate, you should be able to become better at determining which physical symptoms need to be focused on.
- When you time your emotions, you need to understand your own personal emotional time structure. If you are in a bad mood, you typically know that you are going to be able to rid yourself of this mood by a certain time. This is not always going to be true, but it is worthwhile to form some sort of structure for your emotions. Try to learn your timeline, and see if you can work through them long enough for them to dissipate.
- Everybody has something that is going to trigger them to no end. Even when you are feeling very emotionally strong, this triggering emotion can cause a setback if you allow it to. The thing to remember is that you have the power here. You get to decide if you are going to be set back by this or if you are going to rise above it and move forward. Once you can

identify this particular trigger, then you are going to have all of the power over it.

- Instead of trying to invalidate yourself or to eliminate your emotions entirely, you need to teach yourself that it is okay to feel the way that you are feeling. This will rewire your brain by reminding you that what you feel is important, and you do not have to change who you are just because of what society thinks about you or your actions. Show yourself that feeling emotions is normal, and working through them is an action of strength.

These are the main points for you to remember as you work on your emotional clarifying journey. This is a journey because it is going to continue to evolve over time. You are going to grow as a person, and this can change the entire way that you feel about certain situations or events. The things that used to bother you in the past might not affect you at all in the present. You never know what this means for your future, as well. For this reason, you need to keep an open mind and be gentle on yourself as you work through this.

Why This Benefits You

You want to be a go-getter mom and the best mom that you can be. You want to be able to have a wonderful and successful career while also raising a family. Anything that benefits you is worth the time and energy that you need to put into it. The ability to understand where your emotions come from will benefit you in many ways. Not only will it make your days easier but it will also end up making your life easier in the process. These steps that you take are very big steps toward self-healing.

Happiness Is Linked to Clarity

When you think about it, the happiest you have ever been is when you have been extremely clear about your emotions and what you are feeling. Your happiness is directly related to the emotional clarity that you can obtain for yourself. Most people would argue that the purpose of life is to figure out how to live as happily as possible. If this is something that you are striving for, then clarifying your emotions is definitely going to help you reach this end goal.

Everybody wants more happiness, but they do not always know where to find it. You can find it through clarity if you give it a chance. Take note of how much better you feel when your head is clear and free of complex emotions. Once you begin processing them, it is almost like the noise in your head starts to quiet down. You can then focus on what is most important to you and what you need to do to keep this happiness going.

Being happy is not always a simple task. You might have a wonderful family and a great job, but it is still normal to feel unhappy at times. Your emotions can change your mood at the drop of a hat, but you already know that you do not have to stay in this negativity for a long time. You can regain your clarity and understand how to get back to the happiest point in your life.

Using happiness as your motivation is great because you want it—everybody does. There is no reason why you should turn away additional happiness in your life whenever possible because you deserve it. You have been working so hard lately, and you always deserve nothing but the best. Teach yourself that this is true by repeating the mantra frequently. Repeat it to yourself in the mirror.

Visualization Can Help You

Visualization is a technique that you may or may not have tried already. It is similar to meditation, but it involves imagination. All that you must do is take a quiet moment alone, close your eyes, and visualize your ideal life or situation. See what comes to your mind first, and go with this thought. See what you can make of this narrative by paying attention to what it will teach you. Visualize yourself reaching your end goal, and think about how happy this is going to make you.

The more you visualize, the more your brain is going to believe that it's going to be true. This is something that is psychological, and it will prove to you that you can change your entire mindset by simply thinking more positively. Focus on what it is that you want and need in life. When you imagine what you want out of life and what you need to do, you are going to feel like you are making progress on a regular basis. This is going to allow you to feel fulfilled and successful.

Visualization also benefits you because you are able to take yourself out of any active negative situations that you might be presently going through. You are transporting yourself to a better place that is more positive. This is going to allow you to act in a more productive manner, and you will feel proud of yourself overall for doing so. Visualization can be a great relaxation technique. It will calm you down, even during your most stressful moments in life. Believe in it as you work through it. The more seriously you take the process, the better it will work for you.

Negative Emotions Can Trigger Other Negative Emotions

Negative emotions can feel like a domino effect when they are left on their own to fester. When you begin to submit to your negative emotions, you are going to feel plenty of other emotions begin to flood in. This does not have to result in such a dramatic end result if you are able to control these emotions. When you can feel yourself spiraling, this is a sign that you must regroup. Think about what you are doing and why you are deciding to do it. Ask yourself if this spiral is going to benefit you in any way. Likely, it is not.

You do not have to be owned by your negative emotions because you are a lot more powerful than you think. The more that you work with them, the more this benefits you because you will realize your true power. You will see exactly what you are capable of in ways that you might have been unaware of before. You can do this, and you can do anything that you set your mind to! This is the point of visualization and using the exercise to clear your head.

Make sure that you are patient with yourself during this entire process. It is not going to change overnight, and you are not going to be able to simply visualize something that you want while truly believing that it can happen for you. This is something that can take time, but you must be willing to give it the proper time for it to start working. Teach yourself that good things come to those who wait, and this definitely involves your emotions and all that come with them.

When you can feel that you are getting triggered, try your best to step away from the situation if you can. See if you can physically take some space to just breathe through whatever it is you are feeling. You already have an idea of the timeline of these negative emotions because you have learned so much. With a little bit of time to breathe, you will be able to regroup.

By thinking about these benefits and how they are going to change your life, feel proud of yourself for making it to this point. Even though you are so busy taking care of your family and your tasks at work, you still made the time to learn more about these benefits. You are doing a great job, and you are going to be rewarded immensely for this.

CONCLUSION

Take a look at yourself and all that you have learned—this is a great accomplishment! You already knew how to be an excellent and caring mother who is always there for your children. Before this book, you knew how to get your work done in a precise and timely manner. Now, you have even more skills to use in life that will allow you to become even better. You are a wonderful and courageous woman, and you need to tell yourself this on a regular basis until you believe it. By learning that you do not have to do it all—that you can delegate tasks and ask for help—you are going to realize that you can get more done than ever before.

This is going to result in a lot more happiness and motivation to complete your personal and professional goals. By finding your true purpose in life, you are going to be able to live by your priorities in a way that gives you something to look forward to each day. You will see that you do not just have to go with the mundane routine that you are used to completing. You can create your own routine that is much more fulfilling and productive.

If at any point someone doubts you, remember that they are not living your life. They do not know what you have been through, what you are going through, and what amazing plans you have for your future. This is a personal journey that you do not have to share with everybody if it feels too private. Share it with those who will support you, and focus the rest of your energy on the tasks that it takes to get there. You are going to be glad that you preserved it in this way and feel even more pleased with yourself than you already do.

With the tools you have learned in this book, you now have a great grasp on how to set clear boundaries both at home and at work. You know how to clarify your emotions and why this is so important for your mental health. You even understand how to identify your physical symptoms to determine if the stress is causing them or if you just need a little extra self-care when you get some alone time. These are all powerful tools and concepts that you can now rely on to help you, even through your hardest moments.

Tell yourself each day that you are a wonderful mother and a great employee—you can definitely be both of these simultaneously. Listen to the praise that you receive from your family and your superiors at work. This is going to keep you motivated and moving in the right direction. Even when you feel like you have fallen short, you can remind yourself that you are still doing a great job by taking a look back at all of the wonderful progress you have made. Allow yourself to be proud of yourself!

REFERENCES

Athuraliya, A. (2021, May 14). *How to write an action plan: Step-by-step guide with templates.* Creately Blog. https://creately.com/blog/diagrams/how-to-write-an-action-plan/.

Castrillon, C. (2020, July 3). *10 Ways to set healthy boundaries at work.* Forbes. https://www.forbes.com/sites/carolinecastrillon/2019/07/18/10-ways-to-set-healthy-boundaries-at-work/?sh=7268a4c87497.

Davis, T. (n.d.). *Emotional clarity.* The Berkeley Well-Being Institute. https://www.berkeleywellbeing.com/emotional-clarity.html.

Emotional clarity: 6 Key principles for managing your emotions. Nick Wignall. (2020, June 9). https://nickwignall.com/emotional-clarity/.

Fader, S. (2019, September 8). *Being a career woman and a mother: how to find balance.* Betterhelp. https://www.betterhelp.com/advice/careers/being-a-career-woman-and-a-mother-how-to-find-balance/.

Forman, T. (2019, April 30). *How to be a great mom and have a great career.* Forbes. https://www.forbes.com/sites/tamiforman/2017/08/02/can-you-have-a-great-career-and-be-a-great-mom/?sh=747d24f269ab.

How moms can accept help from others. Raising Bliss // Enjoying Motherhood. (2021, June 7). https://raisingbliss.com/how-moms-can-accept-help-from-others/.

Locke, M. (2020, August 1). *How to set boundaries as a mom*. Michelle Locke. https://www.writingbetweenpauses.com/blog/how-to-set-boundaries-as-a-mom.

Morin, A. (2015, April 21). *5 Ways to stop giving negative people too much power in your life*. Forbes. https://www.forbes.com/sites/amymorin/2015/01/10/5-ways-to-stop-giving-negative-people-too-much-power-in-your-life/?sh=784f65c970c7.

Morin, A. (2020, July 13). *7 Ways to find more meaning and purpose in your life*. Verywell Mind. https://www.verywellmind.com/tips-for-finding-your-purpose-in-life-4164689.

Rao, T. (2021, January 27). *Personal and professional goals: What's the difference and how to set them*. Pure Healthy Living. https://purehealthyliving.com/blog/personal-and-professional-goals-whats-the-difference-and-how-to-set-them#:~:text=Professional%20goals%20are%20related%20to,relationships%2C%20and%20well%2Dbeing.

The 4 Ds of Time Management. (n.d.). ProductPlan. https://www.productplan.com/glossary/4-ds-of-time-management/.

The Muse. (2020, June 19). *13 Ways the busiest people ever avoid burnout*. The Muse. https://www.themuse.com/advice/13-ways-the-busiest-people-ever-avoid-burnout.

Van Edwards, V. (2020, April 20). *8 Ways to achieve greatness*. Science of People. https://www.scienceofpeople.com/achieve-greatness/.

Ziegler, S. (2021, May 27). *7 Signs you're suffering from working mommy burnout-and what to do about it*. Working Mother. https://www.workingmother.com/7-signs-youre-suffering-from-working-mommy-burnout-and-what-to-do-about-it.

www.ingramcontent.com/pod-product-compliance
Lightning Source LLC
Chambersburg PA
CBHW050323010526
44119CB00003B/79